# Consumer Behaviour
# in
# North East India

# Consumer Behaviour in North East India

James L.T. Thanga

ANSHAH
Anshah Publishing House

ISBN: 978-81-8364-073-2

First Published in India in 2010

*Consumer Behaviour in North East India*



*Published by:*
**ANSHAH PUBLISHING HOUSE**
H.O.: LG 18-19, Pankaj Central Market, Patparganj,
I.P. Ext., Delhi-110092, Tel: 91-11-2223 5152, 2223 6152
Br.Off.: 4617/18, Ansari Road, Darya Ganj,
New Delhi-110002, Tel: 6594 6453, 9810522367
E-mail: info@shiprapublications.com
www.shiprapublications.com

*Dedicated to*

*My father Dengchungnunga,*
*mother Zochhingpuii,*
*wife Sangpuii,*
*and*
*daughter Losis.*

# Preface

Study of consumer behaviour, being the fundamental aspect of economic activities, occupied a prominent place in empirical studies right from the later part of the 19th century. It focuses on the allocation of scarce resources to various goods and services by individual or group of individual consumers. The attainments of basic necessities of life by each person in the countries can be ascertained from the level of per capita consumer expenditure. As such, consumer expenditure is a good measure of standard of living of the people. An increase in total per capita consumer expenditure at constant prices becomes the good indicator of the improvement of standard of living.

One important aspect in the study of consumer behaviour is to estimate various price elasticties and expenditure (income) elasticity from the estimated of individual's or household's consumption of goods and services to changes in price and income, and forecasting of future demand. Various estimated elasticcities are good information to policy makers. Another aspect in the study of consumer behaviour is the estimation of consumption function, which is consumption-income relationship. The estimated consumption function can be used to measure marginal propensity to consume and marginal propensity to save which is useful information to estimate the impact of investment on income generation in the economy.

An attempt is made in this book to study the consumer behaviour in North East India using the State of Mizoram as a case study. An attempt is made in this study to review some of the previous studies, to analyze the general pattern of consumer expenditure in North East India, to measure the inequalities in income and consumption, to make a comparative analysis of consumer behaviour by estimating expenditure elasticities for both rural and urban areas of Mizoram.

I received many advices, encouragements and helps from friends and colleagues My sincere thanks go to Prof. Thangehungnunga, Head,

Department of Economics. Mizoram University for his scholarly guidance, untiring help and encouragement; Prof. Tlanglawma, Director. Academic Staff College, Mizoram University for his effective suggestions and encouragements.

I wish to give special acknowledgements to Mrs. H. Rosangpuii (my wife), who typed much of the manuscript and was supportive, shared my anxieties and concerns throughout my study. I also express my deep gratitude to my father Dengehungnunga and my mother Zochhingpuii, for their unending support and inspiration throughout my academic career.

Above all, I deeply thank almighty God who has showered me with blessing, mental faculty and sound health.

Aizawl **James L.T. Thanga**
29th May, 2010

# Contents

# List of Tables

# 1
# Introduction

Consumption economics is a branch of economics that focuses on consumer's behaviour as they allocate economic resources to satisfy their wants. Consumption economists make use of a generally accepted or standard body of economic theory about the behaviour of individual consumers and some theory pertinent to total or aggregate consumption for a large group of people, as in a whole country. In addition, researchers and economists carry on empirical investigation resulting into basic understandings about consumption trends and variations emerge from this research. Consumption economics focuses on economic behaviour and economic phenomena, i.e. on the allocation of scarce resources and on the value of goods and services purchased by individual consumers and by groups of consumers.

Consumption economics has been evolving from two lines of economic theory; microeconomic theory of consumer behaviour and macroeconomic theory related consumption behaviour.

## 1.1 MICROECONOMIC THEORY OF CONSUMER BEHAVIOUR

Economic theory of consumer behaviour was synthesized by Alfred Marshall towards the end of the 19th century from the ideas of the classical economists and the proponents of the marginal utility. Marshall identified consumption with the relationship between consumer choice making and the determination of market prices. At the same time, attention had been given to the relationship effect of family income on consumer behaviour at micro level towards the end of the 19th century.

The concept of utility is basic to the standard theory of consumer behaviour, and most of the formal economics of consumption is built on it. As empirical economics and the science of psychology developed, the impossibility of measuring utility in cardinal numbers caused a cardinal utility explanation of consumer behaviour to lose favour. An ordering approach, caused indifferences analysis, has gained much favour, especially since J.R. Hicks gave it new impetus by his 1939 exposition in value and capital.

Microeconomic approach consists of two well-known studies: family budget data analysis and market demand analysis. Family budget analysis deals with the cross-section relationship between income levels and the pattern of consumption as across categories of goods and services holding other variables constant. The first well-known family budget analysis was done by Ernst Engel in 1857. The market demand analysis, on the other hand, uses time-series data to analyze the price-demand relationship.

The microeconomic theory of demand has been, systematically, analyzed by economists such as Allen (1935), Hicks (1939) and Samuelson (1947). Empirical investigation has been undertaken to test the theories by several economists such as Schultz (1938), Wold (1943-44 and 1953), Stone (1954), Prais and Houthakker (1955), Houthakker (1957) and others. Family budget analysis generally involved in the estimation of Engel's Curves and the corresponding expenditure elasticities for various groups of commodities. In India, most of the studies on consumption behaviour have been concentrated on estimation of expenditure elasticities for different groups of items using cross-sectional data. Estimation and analysis of expenditure elasticities in India have been done by several Indian economists like Iyengar, *et al.* (1960 and 1968), Sinha (1966), Gupta (1968), Coondoo (1969 and 1975), Singh and Singh (1971), Upender (1998), Prasad (2001).

## 1.2 MACROECONOMIC THEORY OF CONSUMPTION

The subdivision of economics into micro and macro theory is largely a Post-World War II development. Before 1940 most economic theory pertinent to consumption by large groups of people, as for example, the entire population was developed from the theory of behaviour of an individual consumer by direct generalization. What the individual consumer would do in response to price alternatives or income changes was assumed to hold true for all consumers in a market or country. This assumption ignored differences among individuals and a variety of problems in summing or aggregating over many people and often over several slightly different products. Aggregate consumption has featured in macro-models since Keynes (1936). Keynes postulated the consumption function as the relationship between consumption and disposable income. Macroeconomic approach concentrates on the income-consumption relationship in aggregative form.

The theoretical work of Keynes on the consumption function led to the statistical estimation of the propensity to consume by Kuznets (1946) and Goldsmith (1955). Inspired by the findings of Kuznets and Goldsmith, several economists tried to refine aggregate consumption theory. The most influential attempt on the refinement of Keynesian consumption function had been made by Duessenberry (1949), Friedman (1957), Brumberg, Modigliani and Ando (1954, 1963). At the same time, the consumption function of India have been estimated and analyzed by several Indian economists like Narasimham (1956), Iyengar and Moorthy (1959), Roy Choudhury (1968), Gupta (1970), Mammon (1982)

## 1.3 PATTERN OF CONSUMER EXPENDITURE IN INDIA

According to the 62nd NSS Round in 2005-06, nearly 19 per cent of the Indian rural population belonged to households with monthly per capita consumption expenditure (MPCE) less than Rs. 365 that is, spending less than Rs. 12 per person per day on consumption, at 2005-06 prices. For rural Orissa and Chhattisgarh, the percentage of population with such low consumption expenditure levels was as high as 44 per cent. For Madhya Pradesh, Jharkhand and Bihar, the percentage was in the range 29-34 per cent. In urban India, where expenditure levels were higher, 22 per cent of the population belonged to households with monthly per capita expenditure less than Rs. 580 (about Rs. 19 per person per day). In urban Bihar, 56 per cent of the urban populations were in this category. In urban Orissa and Uttar Pradesh, the percentage was 36-38 per cent, and in all other major States it was under 30 per cent. Average monthly per capita consumer expenditure (average MPCE) in 2005-06 was Rs. 625 in rural India and Rs. 1171 in urban India at 2005-06 prices.

In 2005-06, on the average, rural Indian spent 53 per cent of their total expenditure on food; while urban Indian spend 40 per cent on food. Value of average food consumption per person in urban areas was within the range Rs. 451-Rs. 500 per month in 7 out of 17 major States. In respect of rural food consumption, 13 major States belonged to the range Rs. 251-400. In rural India, the share of food in total consumer expenditure varied from 44 per cent in Punjab and Kerala to 60 per cent in Assam and 61 per cent in Bihar and Jharkhand. In urban India the share of food was 51 per cent in Bihar and 36-45 per cent in all other major States.

Rural and urban households differed little in the share of the budget allocated to fuel and light (10% for rural, 9% for urban), clothing, including bedding and footwear (7% for rural, 6% for urban), and medical care (7% for rural, 6% for urban). Rural and urban households differed noticeably in the share of the budget allocated to cereals (17% for rural, 10% for urban), rent (less than 0.5% for rural, 6% for urban), education (3% for rural, 6% for urban), and miscellaneous consumer services including transport and telephone (8% for rural, 14% for urban).

## 1.3 SCOPE

Empirical study of consumption behaviour generally has three aspects: one, the estimation and analysis of Engel's Curves and the corresponding expenditure elasticities of demand for various items of consumption; two, estimation of demand function and price elasticities of demand; and three, the estimation of aggregate consumption function and the corresponding propensities to consume. Due to the limited availability of time series data on price and quantity demanded for various selected commodity groups for analysis, we do not cover market demand analysis in this book. Accordingly, the study of consumption behaviour in this book used Engel's Law and Keynesian Absolute Income Hypothesis and the subsequent development of consumption function as the underpinning theoretical assumptions. Side by side with the estimated propensities to consume, the saving propensities have been estimated.

## 1.4 RELEVANCE

The relevance of the study of consumption behaviour arises from the special circumstances of the developing nations like India. The present work analyses the consumption function as applied to the estimation of various expenditure elasticities from the cross-section data of Mizoram state. The estimates of expenditure elasticities are relevant for the producers of various goods and services in the economy. The producers can increase or reduce the quantity of their production according to the projection of demand for the commodities by the estimated consumption function (or Engel's function) or expenditure elasticities. Hence, the estimates can be a basis for the production decision in the economy.

For the government, especially in a developing country, which is trying to secure self-sufficiency in food production, the estimate of consumption function or expenditure elasticity for food items is quite relevant. Projection of future food demand would enable the government to allocate resources to meet the future requirement of its food demand in the economy. Estimates of expenditure elasticities would enable us to identify various commodities into necessity, semi-luxury and luxury items in the state. This would help the government to achieve its policy of reducing inequality through taxation. Thus, the government can formulate more efficient and effective tax policy to reduce tax burden of the poor.

The estimate of aggregate consumption function is helpful to predict the saving potential of the economy with the changing level of income. Knowledge of future levels of savings will enable the government to decide on the precise investment policies to increase the rate of growth of the economy. Further, estimated propensities to consume can be used to determine or estimate the possible impact of developmental activities undertaken by the government on the income generation and the standard of living through the working of multiplier.

In addition to the estimates of expenditure elasticities for various commodities and marginal propensities, the analysis of the trend of per capita expenditure in NER would enable us to asses the improvement of standard of living in the region. It will also reveal the growing inequalities of rural and urban areas, and inequalities of income and consumption among the people. This will enable the government to pursue right policy measure to achieve an all time objective of growth with social justice.

## 1.5 OBJECTIVES

The analysis of consumption behaviour on the basis of the fitted Engel's curves helps us in classifying various food and nonfood items as necessities, luxuries and semi-luxuries which would indirectly enable us to asses the aspects of the consumers in NER and in Mizoram in particular regarding their habits, tastes and preferences. The study of consumption behaviour has been made with the following objectives:

(i) To analyze the trend of per capita consumer expenditure, the standard of living by implication, in North-Eastern Region along with the growing rural-urban disparities in income and consumption.

(ii) To review the general patterns of consumer expenditure in various states of NER.

(iii) To classify the various consumption items of the people in Mizoram into necessities, luxuries and semi-luxuries by estimating their respective expenditure elasticities.

(iv) To examine the extent of class difference between various monthly consumers expenditure (MPCE) classes in consumption of various commodities in Mizoram as well as the extent of inequalities in consumption or income.

(v) To examine the rural-urban difference in the consumption behaviour on various goods and services.

(vi) To study the saving behaviour side by side with the estimated aggregate consumption behaviour in Mizoram.

## 1.6 HYPOTHESES

Proposed hypotheses to be tested in this study are the following:

(i) Consumption expenditure increases with an increase in income, but less than proportionately.

(ii) The proportion of expenditure spent on food decreases as the consumer's expenditure increases.

(iii) There is a significant difference in the consumption behaviour between rural and urban areas.

(iv) Saving is the rising function of income. In other words, as income increases the rate of saving also increases.

## 1.7 METHODOLOGY

### 1.7.1 Collection of Empirical Data

Data used in the present study is primarily based on the sample survey conducted in Mizoram by the author during July-August 2007. In the process of generating empirical data on this survey, the method of multi-stage sampling was adopted for both rural and urban areas. Multi-stage sampling consists of the selection of sample from each stage on a simple random basis.

In rural areas, a randomly selected 4 Rural Development (RD) Blocks constitutes the first-stage units. From these 4 Blocks, 11 villages were selected to constitute the second-stage sampling units. From these selected villages, 179 households were selected as the ultimate-sampling units. The required information was obtained from each of this household through schedule questionnaires and direct interview with the respondent. The survey covered 1093 person from 179 rural households.

In urban areas, on the other hand, 5 urban towns out of 23 towns (including Aizawl city) were selected to constitute the first-stage units. From these towns, 193 households were selected as the final sampling units. The required information was obtained from each of the selected household. The survey covered 4 urban towns and 1193 person from 193 households. Details of the villages, towns and number of households covered in the study are given in Table 1.1.

Secondary data on household consumption expenditure are obtained from the reports of various rounds of National Sample Survey (NSS), Ministry of Statistic and Programme Implementation, Government of India. To find the latest data for all states of North-Eastern Region, we tabulate the ungroup data of the 62nd NSS Round which cover the period of 2005-06.

**Table 1.1:** Number of Households and Persons Covered in the Sample Survey of July-August, 2007

<table>
<tr><th colspan="3">Urban Areas</th><th colspan="4">Rural Areas</th></tr>
<tr><th>City/Town</th><th>No. of Sampled Households</th><th>No. of Persons Covered</th><th>Villages</th><th>RD Block</th><th>No. of Sampled Households</th><th>No. of Persons Covered</th></tr>
<tr><td>Aizawl</td><td>86</td><td>496</td><td>Reiek</td><td>Reiek</td><td>19</td><td>101</td></tr>
<tr><td>Lunglei</td><td>46</td><td>251</td><td>Rawpuichhip</td><td>-do-</td><td>19</td><td>104</td></tr>
<tr><td>Serchhip</td><td>29</td><td>184</td><td>Ailawng</td><td>-do-</td><td>13</td><td>58</td></tr>
<tr><td>Mamit</td><td>20</td><td>122</td><td>East Lungdar</td><td>E. Lungdar</td><td>20</td><td>124</td></tr>
<tr><td>Saiha</td><td>12</td><td>66</td><td>N. Mualcheng</td><td>-do-</td><td>22</td><td>135</td></tr>
<tr><td>Urban Total</td><td>193</td><td>1119</td><td>Bawktlang</td><td>-do-</td><td>24</td><td>144</td></tr>
<tr><td colspan="3" rowspan="7">1. Number of households covered in the survey: 372.<br>2. Number of persons covered in the survey: 2212.</td><td>Saikah</td><td>Lawngtlai</td><td>20</td><td>124</td></tr>
<tr><td>Mampui</td><td>-do-</td><td>7</td><td>38</td></tr>
<tr><td>Thingkah</td><td>-do-</td><td>15</td><td>111</td></tr>
<tr><td>N.E. Khawdungsei</td><td>NGOPA</td><td>11</td><td>83</td></tr>
<tr><td>Chiahpui</td><td>-do-</td><td>9</td><td>71</td></tr>
<tr><td>Rural Total</td><td></td><td>179</td><td>1093</td></tr>
</table>

As far as the per capita income of the state is concerned, the required information are obtained from Economic Survey published by Ministry of Statistics and Programme Implementation, Government of India, Statistical Handbook of Mizoram published by the directorate of

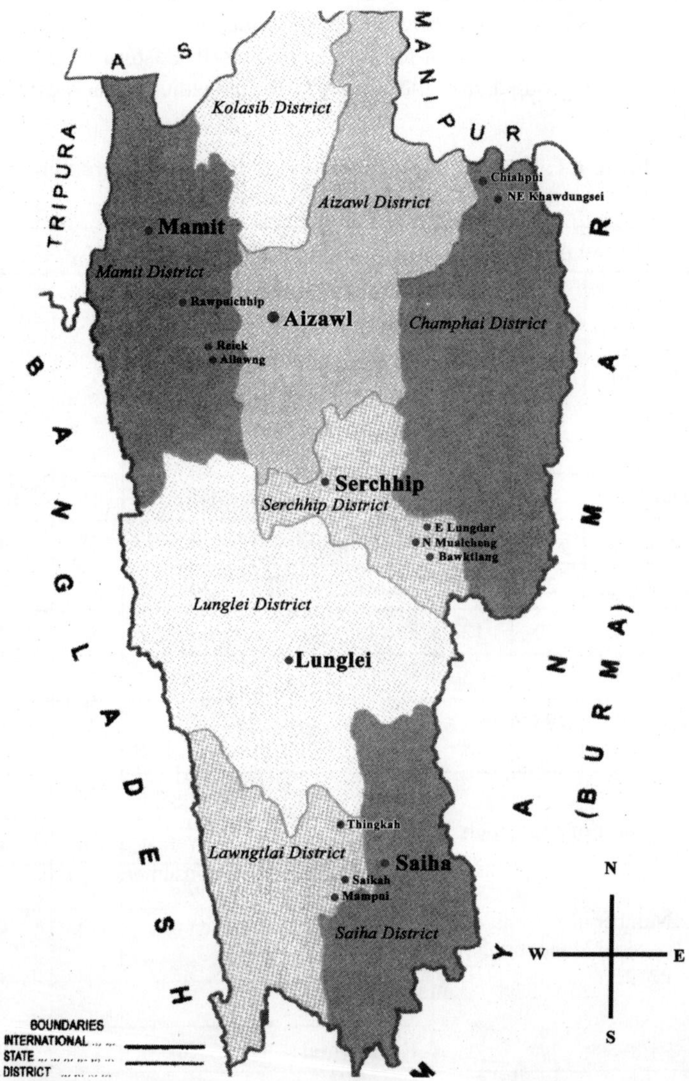


Geographical Location of Sample Villages/Town/City

Economics and Statistics, Government of Mizoram and the Basic Statistics of North-Eastern Region published by North-Eastern Council, Ministry of Home Affairs, Govt. of India. The series of Wholesale Price Indices for Food and Nonfood items are obtained from the 'Wholesale Price Index, Published by Economic Advisory Council, Ministry of Industries, Government of India. In addition to these, the required data are generated from various sources like Reports of Population Census, Published and unpublished articles, etc.

### 1.8.2 Classification of Household Consumer Expenditure Data

In the sample survey conducted during July-August, 2007, household expenditures are obtained from two broad household items of consumption, namely, expenditure on food items and non-food items. Food item includes (a) beverages, (b) meat, (c) vegetables, (d) cereals, salt, sugar and edible oils. Similarly, non-food item includes (a) pan, tobacco and intoxicants, (b) health care, (c) entertainments and telecommunication, (d) clothing and housing, (e) education, (f) transportation, and (g) miscellaneous. The total monetary value of the household monthly consumption on each of the item divided by household size gives the total monthly per capita expenditure (MPCE).

The expenditure on each of the item is estimated on the basis of its consumption during the reference period. Reference periods are allotted to different items on the basis of the length of time on which the consumption can be recalled.

### 1.8.3 Methods of Analysis

The data so collected in the survey are analyzed and compared using regression technique, Analysis of Variance (ANOVA) technique, Analysis of Covariance (ANOCOVA) technique and the Chow Test.

The present study considered per capita monthly consumer expenditure and its dis-aggregation into broad expenditure groups. The Ordinary Least Squares (OLS) method is used for estimation of regression equations. Parameters are estimated by using linear and log-linear Engel's functions. Using the estimated parameters of Engel's functions, we finally calculate the expenditure elasticities for each group. In the process of estimation of Engel's curves we used the total consumer expenditure as an independent variable. The effect of family sizes on household consumption behaviour have also been analyzed using double-log Engel curve where family size is used as one of the explanatory variables.

The sample households are divided into six Monthly Per Capita Consumer Expenditure (MPCE) classes. Separate regressions for all commodities are estimated in each of the MPCE class. Estimates of regression line represent the consumption behaviour of their respective class. The significance of the difference in consumption behaviour among six classes is tested using the ANOVA technique under the null hypothesis of equal slope (marginal propensity) coefficients for all classes.

Comparative analysis of consumption behaviour between rural and urban areas of Mizoram has been done on the basis of the estimated regressions for both areas. The expenditure elasticities so calculated are used to explain the rural-urban differentials in consumption behaviour. To test the significance of the difference between rural and urban areas, the technique of ANOCOVA has been adopted for all commodities. The null hypothesis underlying ANOCOVA are equal intercept, slope and overall regressions for both areas. Further, the Chow Test has been used to test the equality of marginal propensity to consume for aggregate consumption functions between rural and urban areas of Mizoram.

## 1.9 CONCEPTUAL FRAMEWORKS

The study being made in this book is primarily based on two theories of consumption behaviour, namely, Engel's Law and Consumption Function.

### 1.9.1 Engel's Law

Ernst Engel (1821-96) in 1857[1] published an empirical law concerning the relation between income and expenditure on food on the basis of his study on the conditions of production and consumption in the Kingdom of Saxony and this have become the famous Engel's Law. Engel's Law states that the proportion of income spent on food declines as income rises. Its original statement was mainly based on an examination of about two hundred budgets of Belgian labourers collected by Ducpetiaux (1855)[2]. Since then the law has been found to hold in many other budget surveys; similar laws have been formulated for other items of expenditure (Houthakker, 1957)[3].

Engel used total expenditure as a measure of total purchasing power, rather than income, apparently because of difficulties in obtaining data. The ratio of variations in food expenditure to variation in total expenditure is somewhat lower than the ratio of variation in food expenditure to variation of income because part of the variation in income is taken up by the variation in savings. However, Engel's law is stated in such general term 'income' can be substituted for 'total expenditures' without changing the interpretation.

### 1.9.2 Engel Curve

For any single commodity, the relation between income and consumption can be summarized in a convenient form for statistical determination known as the Engel Curve. A good is called normal if its consumption increases in response to an increase in income and conversely decreases in response to a decrease in income. In the case of normal good, a positive relationship exists between income and consumption; it follows that Engel curve must have a positive slope. On the other hand, a good is called inferior if its consumption decreases in response to an increase in income and vice versa, if it increases in response to a decrease in income. In case of inferior good Engel Curve is negatively sloped.

### 1.9.3 Engel Curve and Income Elasticity of Demand

The income elasticity is defined as the proportionate change in the quantity demanded resulting from a proportionate change in income. It is the measure of the degree of sensitivity of consumer purchase of goods to changes in income of the consumer. The most direct measure of the sensitivity of a consumer's purchase of good X to changes in income Y would be the ratio $\Delta X/\Delta Y$. For small changes, $\Delta X$ and $\Delta Y$, this ratio can be interpreted as the slope of the Engel Curve. We can write this as the derivative $dX/dY$, where the symbol 'd' indicated the effect of varying the underlying parameter. Symbolically, the income elasticity of demand may be written:

$$h = \frac{dQX}{dY} \cdot \frac{Y}{QX} \qquad \text{... (1.1)}$$

The income elasticity is greater than, equal to, or less than unity depending upon whether the slope along the Engel Curve is greater than, equal to, or less than the slope of a ray drawn from the origin to the curve. If income elasticity is negative, the Engel Curve has negative slope.

On the basis of the income elasticity economists divide goods into normal and inferior. Further, Normal goods are subdivided into two sub-groups: just normal and ultra-superior (also known as luxuries). Goods whose income elasticity is between 0 and 1 are just normal; and goods whose income elasticity is greater than 1 are normal, but they are also known as ultra-superior. In summary, we can state:

(i) If the commodity is inferior, income elasticity is negative. Inferior goods are not often encountered. Recent studies of consumers' responses to changes in income indicate that commodities are either normal or ultra-superior

(ii) Goods such as furniture, cars and whisky are ultra-superior. Goods such as food, clothing and transportation are normal in the sense that consumers always increase consumption of these aggregate goods in response to a rise in their incomes.

(iii) If the commodity is just normal, income elasticity is between 0 and 1.

(iv) If he commodity is normal, but also ultra-superior, income elasticity is greater than 1.

### 1.9.4 Various Forms of the Engel Functions

This part attempts to give a brief highlight of the various forms of Engel's functions being used in empirical research. It may not be possible to give all forms of Engel's functions used by economists in different parts of the world, but an attempt is made here to give the most commonly used forms of Engel function in empirical research. The various forms of Engel function being used in empirical research are given in Table 1.2 where '$y$' denote the money expenditure on particular good or service and '$x$' being total income or total expenditure of the consumer.

The choice of particular form of Engel's curves is widely discussed in economic literature, but there is no compromise on what form of Engel's curves is to be used till today. So, the choice of function depends on individual consideration on the basis of goodness of fit, absence of auto-correlation, economic interpretation and computational simplicity.

### 1.9.5 Absolute Income Hypotheses

J.M. Keyes in his book 'The General Theory of Employment, Interest and Money' (1936)[4] stated the relationship between income and consumption as 'men are disposal, as a rule and on the average to increase their consumption as their income increase, but not by as much the increase in their income". The theory of consumption is an integral part of his General Theory. Keynes was concerned only with total consumption, defined as real consumption expenditure for all goods and services. He clearly stated the hypothesis that (a) real consumption expenditure is a

**Table 1.2:** Forms of Engel's Functions

| *Name* | *Functions* | *Estimators of Elasticity* |
|---|---|---|
| Linear | $y = a + bx$ | $b\frac{x}{y}$ |
| Double-log | $\log y = a + b \log x$ | $B$ |
| Quadratic | $y = a + bx + cx^2$ | $bx + 2\frac{x^2}{y}$ |
| Semi-log (a) | $\log y = a + bx$ | $\frac{b}{y}$ |
| Semi-log (b) | $y = a + b \log x$ | $bx$ |
| Inverse | $y = a - b(\frac{1}{x})$ | $\frac{b}{xy}$ |
| Log-inverse | $\log y = a - b\,(1/x)$ | $\frac{b}{x}$ |
| Log-log-inverse | $\log y = a + b \log x - c\,(1/x)$ | $b + \frac{c}{x}$ |
| Double-log (with family size $n$) | $\log y = a + b \log x + \log n$ | *b (partial elasticity w.r.t. x)* *c (partial elasticity w.r.t n)* |

stable function of real income, and (b) The MPC is positive but less than one. Marginal propensity to consume is the ratio of an absolute change in consumption to an absolute change in income.

Keynes also proposed two other hypotheses: the marginal propensity to consume (MPC) is less than average propensity that declines at higher levels of income. The Keynesian short-run consumption function is represented by linear equation $C = a + bY_d$ where $a$>0 and $b$<1 (i.e. MPC<1).

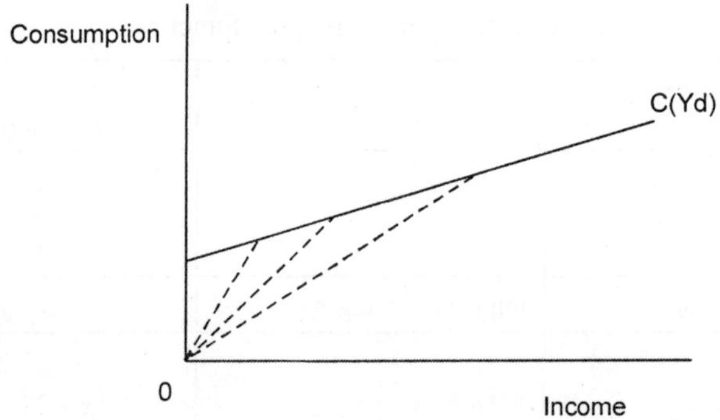


**Fig. 1.1**

In Figure 1.1, 'b' is the slope of the consumption function (C) or MPC and the slope of the dotted lines drawn from the origin to the consumption function indicate the average propensities to consume (APC) which decrease at higher levels of income. Further, it can be seen from the diagram that the cross-section results of APC>MPC is being realized in the Keynes' Absolute Income Hypotheses.

The Keynesian consumption function, typified in Figure 1, fits admirably two kinds of empirical data. First, economy-wide time series of consumption and income for the period between the two world wars (i.e. 1914-1939) lie along the function of the Keynesian type. Secondly, any cross-section survey of household budget appears to confirm Keynesian Psychological Law at a microeconomic level. After World War II, however, several pieces of evidence cast doubt on the Keynesian consumption function. The reappraisal that followed led to new theories and deeper empirical investigation of the determinants of household consumption. First, extrapolations of statistical consumption functions based on prewar US data to potential postwar income levels greatly underestimated the postwar propensity to consume. Secondly, just as the interwar Keynesian consumption function forecasts too much savings after World War II, it 'back casts' too little saving before World War I.

Recognition of these facts led a number of investigators to formulate and test hypotheses that would explain the above defects and success—broadly speaking, hypotheses that would reconcile the short-run, or cyclical, success of the Keynesian consumption function with its long-run or secular failure. In the early 1940's Samuelson (1943) proposed a 'ratchet' model which stated that consumption grows in the long-run roughly in proportion to income; but during cyclical interruptions of long-run growth, consumers defend living standards already attained, and consequently consumption follows a flatter (lower MPC) Keynesian path. Following the work of Samuelson, several economists including Duessenberry, Modigliani and Friedman started new theories and hypotheses that are discussed separately in the following section.

### 1.9.6 The Relative Income Hypotheses

Duessenberry (1949)[5] proposed the relative income hypothesis to reconcile the long run and short-run consumption function. According to this Hypothesis, relative rather than absolute income is the basis for the consumer spending-saving decision. His analysis is based on two relative hypotheses: The first hypotheses is essentially that consumers are not so much concerned with their absolute level of consumption as they are with their consumption relative to the rest of the population. 'Current consumption standards or desires are influenced by other people's consumption behaviour, and desires for future consumption will be influenced in the same way' (Duessenberry, 1949)[6]. This leads to the result that the individual's consumption-income ratio (C/Y) would depend on his position in the income distribution. A person with an income below the average will tend to have a high C/Y ratio, because he is trying to keep up to a national average consumption standard with a below average income. On the other hand, an individual with an above average income will have a lower C/Y ratio.

The second hypothesis is that merely present levels of an absolute and relative income do not influence the present consumption, but also the levels of consumption attained in previous periods. It can also be stated that the ratio of saving to disposable income ($S/Y_d$) to be the function of current disposable income relative to the highest (peak) disposable income $Y_d^*$. If in some period t, for instance, disposable income at time t were to fall below previous peak level, consumers would defend their consumption by reducing savings and ($S_t/Y_{dt}$) would fall. On the other hand, if $Y_{dt}$ were to rise at a relatively steady rate consumption would progressively adjust itself to the new high level of disposable income, and $S_t/Y_d$ would be constant. The resulting consumption function may be written in the following form:

$$\frac{S_t}{Y_{dt}} = a\frac{Y_{dt}}{Y_d *} + b \quad \text{(Saving function)} \qquad \dots (1.2)$$

or

$$\frac{C_t}{Y_{dt}} = 1 - \frac{S_t}{Y_d} \quad \text{(Consumption function)} \dots (1.3)$$

$$= 1 - \left( a \frac{Y_{dt}}{Y_d *} + b \right)$$

Where $S_t$ = Personal saving in period t; $Y_{dt}$ = Disposable personal income in period t and $Y_d*$ = Previous peak disposable income.

### 1.9.7. The Permanent-Income Hypothesis

Milton Friedman's (1957)[7] permanent income hypothesis is to the effect that permanent consumption is proportional to permanent income. He argues that observed, current income consists of a transitory component and a permanent component and that observed consumption has comparable parts. Permanent income during a given period cannot be observed but is hypothesized to be the discounted value of wealth expected over a consumer unit's lifetime.

In formal terms, Friedman's permanent income hypothesis is stated by the three equations:

$$Y = Y_p + Y_t \quad \text{... (1.4)}$$

$$C = C_p + C_t \quad \text{... (1.5)}$$

$$C_p = k\,(i, w, u)\,Y_p \quad \text{... (1.6)}$$

Where

$C$ = actual consumption in some time period.

$C_p$ = expected value of consumption or permanent consumption.

$C_t$ = transitory consumption.

$Y$ = actual income in the same time period

$Y_p$ = expected value of income or permanent income

$Y_t$ = transitory income.

Equation (1.6) defines a relation between permanent income and permanent consumption. It specifies that the ratio between them is independent of the size of permanent income but does depend on other variables, in particular: (1) the rate of interest (i) or sets of rates of interest at which the consumer unit can borrow or lend; (2) the relative importance of property and non-property income, symbolized by the ratio of nonhuman wealth to income (w); and (3) the factors determining the consumer's tastes and preferences (u) (Friedman, 1957). Further, permanent income hypothesis is based upon the assumptions: (1) there is no correlation between permanent income and transitory income; (2) there is no correlation between permanent consumption and transitory consumption; and (3) there is no correlation between transitory income and transitory consumption. Symbolically, these assumptions can be stated as $r_{y_t y_p} = r_{c_t c_p} = r_{y_t c_t} = 0$

### 1.9.8 THE LIFE-CYCLE HYPOTHESIS

According to this hypothesis put forward by Ando, Brumberg and Modigliani[8] since the early 1950's, an individual's consumption depends on his life cycle income and the role of saving is to even out fluctuations in the income stream of the individual during his lifetime. The typical income pattern over an individual's lifetime would be a low level in the early years of life, which rises steadily and attains a peak around middle age and thereafter declines to relatively low levels again during the closing years of his life. The reason for this is that an individual's productivity curve also follows a similar pattern: relatively low productivity levels in the beginning and end of his life.

To explain the long run stability of the average propensity to consume, Ando and Modigliani (1963)[9] build a model of consumption based on several assumptions. If the population distribution by age and income is relatively constant, and taste between present and future consumption are stable through time, we can add up all the individual consumption functions to a stable function, i.e.

$$C_t = K(PV_t) = K\left(\sum \frac{Yt}{(1+r)^t}\right) \qquad \text{... (1.7)}$$

Where C is consumption; Y is income; the lower case t indicate time period; and k is the fraction of consumers' Present Value of future income (PV) that they want to consume in period t.

Income is classified into two categories—labour income ($Y_L$) and property income ($Y_p$). The present value of income in the current time period can then be written as:

$$PV_0 = \sum_0^T \frac{Y_{tL}}{(1+r)^t} + \sum_0^T \frac{Y_{tp}}{(1+r)^t} \qquad \text{... (1.8)}$$

The present value of the property income is assumed to be equal to the value of the property itself at the beginning of the current period. Also the current labour income that is known is isolated from the expected future labour income. These two considerations make:

$$PV_0 = Y_{0L} + \sum_1^T \frac{Y_{tL}}{(1+r)^t} + a_0$$

But the average expected future labour income in time 0 ( $Y_0^L$ ) is given by:

$$Y_0^L = \frac{\sum_{1}^{T} \frac{Y_{tL}}{(1+r)^t}}{T-1}$$

Therefore,

$$\sum_{1}^{T} \frac{Y_{tL}}{(1+r)^t} = (T-1)\ Y_0^L \quad \text{... (1.9)}$$

where T–1 is the average remaining life expectation of the population. And hence,

$$PV_0 = Y_0^L + (T-1)\ Y_0^L \quad \text{... (1.10)}$$

Further, to relate average expected future labour income to current labour income, Ando and Modigliani assumed that the former is some multiple of the latter: That is,

$$Y_0^e = \beta\ Y_0^L;\ \beta > 0 \quad \text{... (1.11)}$$

We then have

$$PV_0 = Y_0^L + (T-1)\ \beta Y_0^L + a_0 = [1+\beta\,(T-1)]\ Y_0^L + a_0$$

This gives

$$C_0 = k[1+\beta\,(T-1)]\ Y_0^L + ka_0 \text{ and}$$
$$C_t = k[1+\beta\,(T-1)]\ Y_t^L + ka_t$$
$$\therefore \quad C_t = \alpha\, y_t^L + ka_t \quad (1.12)$$

Where $\alpha = k[1 + \beta\,(T-1)]$

Dividing both sides of the above equation by $Y_t$, we get

$$\frac{C_t}{Y_t} = a\frac{Y_{tL}}{Y_t} + k\frac{at}{Y_t} \quad \text{... (1.13)}$$

Hence, $S_t/Y_t = 1 - C_t/Y_t$ will remain constant if $C_t/Y_t$ remains constant. And $C_t/Y_t$ will remain constant if $Y_t^L/Y_t$ the share of labour in the total income and $a_t/Y_t$, the ratio of assets to income remains more or less constant.

The Ando-Modigliani consumption function also explains the short run fluctuations in consumption. In the short run, assets may be assumed to remain constant. Hence, during a recession, the ratio $a_t/Y_t$ will rise and hence $C_t/Y_t$ will also rise. Conversely, during a period of prosperity $a_t/Y_t$ will fall and hence so will $C_t/Y_t$.

The Life Cycle hypothesis thus explains all the three observed phenomena regarding consumption: that MPC<APC in cross section studies; that MPC<APC during business cycles; that APC is constant in the long run. In addition, the hypothesis also brings out the relation between wealth and saving.

### 1.9.9 The New Theories of the Consumption Function

In addition to the above three hypothesis, the literature of consumption function occupied one of the most important places in economic research. The new theories of the consumption function include the *Normal Income Hypotheses*, the *Proportionality Hypotheses* and the *Rate of Growth Hypotheses*. However, the dates and persons are misleading, as these theories were circulated in mimeograph and widely discussed as early as 1953 (Farrell, 1959)[10].

The Normal Income Hypothesis attempts to clarify the vagueness of the basis of new theories that the consumption in a year not only depends on the income in that year but on the life span resources in order to maximize the utility rationally. But future is always uncertain and rational behaviour in uncertainty seems misleading. The hypothesis is that the current income (y) of a consumer affects consumption (c) through its effect on normal income ($\gamma$). Proportionality Hypothesis is related with $\beta$, the slope of the consumption function. This theory says that the consumption function would be a straight line passing through the origin. The hypothesis is equivalent to saying that the consumption is proportional to the normal income of an individual consumer. Lastly, the Rate of Growth Hypothesis is pertaining to the long period equilibrium and says that aggregate saving is influenced by the changes in population structure and in per capita real income. In case these factors are readily changing the part of aggregate income saved is proportional to the rate of growth of aggregate real income.

## 1.10 PROFILE OF NORTH-EASTERN INDIA

### 1.10.1 The Land

North-Eastern India, synonymously known as North-Eastern Region (NER), comprises of Arunachal Pradesh, Assam, Manipur, Meghalaya, Mizoram, Nagaland, Sikkim and Tripura. It is lying between 21.57°N-29.30°N latitude and 88°E-97.30°E longitude. It cover the total area of 2,62,179 Sq. Km which is 7.9 per cent of the total land area of the country.

It has a strategic location having international boundaries with Myanmar in the East, China in the North, Bangladesh in the South-West and Bhutan in the North-West. The McMahon line separates North East India from Tibet. This region is connected with the rest of India only through a narrow corridor in North Bengal, having an approximate width of 33 km on the eastern side and 21 km on the western side. This narrow corridor is popularly known as the 'Siliguri neck' or the 'Chicken's neck'.

North East India is mostly hilly; it has plains on both sides of the river Brahmaputra and the Himalayan range around it. The region is of strategic importance for the country on account of the fact that nearly 90 per cent of its borders form India's international boundaries. About 70 per cent of the region is hilly, and the topography varies within each state. Mountains and hills cover most of Arunachal Pradesh, Mizoram, Nagaland, Meghalaya, Sikkim and about half of Tripura, one-fifth of Assam and nine-tenth of Manipur. The plains of the region are mainly made up of separate land masses—the Brahmaputra Valley and the Barak Valley in Assam and the Tripura plains in the South. In Manipur, the valley is small, comprising only about 10 per cent of the total area of the state. The Brahmaputra Valley stretches longitudinally for about 730 km, from North Lakhimpur to Dhubri district in Assam. The Barak Valley, formed by the river Barak and its tributaries covers the districts of Cachar, Karimganj and Hailakandi of South Assam. The Tripura plain is an extension of the Ganga-Brahmaputra plain.

### 1.10.2 Climate

The rainy season in this region generally commences from March and lasts till the middle of October. The total annual rainfall varies significantly in the region. In Khasi and Jaintia Hills, the annual intensity of rainfall reaches the maximum of about 1080-cm around Cherrapunjee and Mawsynram (having highest rainfall in the world). It is significantly low in the rainshadow area of Nagaon district in Assam. About two-thirds of the annual total rainfall occurs during the four monsoon months of June to September.

The North Eastern region has distinct climate variations. The rapid changes in topography result in climate changes within short distance. Generally the daily temperature in the plains of Brahmaputra and the Barak Valley as well as in Tripura and in the western portion of Mizo Hills is about 15°C in January, whereas in other parts of the region, the temperature is between 10°C to 15°C. From April it rises and in July except the south-eastern portion of Mizo hills and Shillong, the mean temperature ranges from 25°C to 27.5°C. During October, daily mean temperature in the hilly areas ranges between 20°C and 25°C, whereas in

Brahmaputra and Barak Valley, Tripurá and the western portion of the Mizo hills it is above 25°C. Further the lowest temperature is experienced below freezing point in the upper Himalayas in Arunachal Pradesh.

### 1.10.3 The People

The region is marked by uneven spatial distribution of population among the constituent states, the primary reason being that the plains and valleys offer more congenial conditions for absorption of population than the hills and difficult terrains. Apart from Assam and Tripura, the NE states are mostly inhabited by tribes having unique social and cultural practices. Overall, tribals (i.e. Schedule Tribe) account for over 26.9 per cent of the total population of this region. However, in Arunachal Pradesh, Meghalaya, Mizoram and Nagaland, scheduled tribes comprise more than 60 per cent of the population. That is what gives these states a predominantly tribal character. The major religions of the people in this region are Hinduism, Islam, Christianity and Buddhism.

**Table 1.3:** Total Population, Land Area, Density, Population of Scheduled Castes and Scheduled Tribes and Their Proportions to the Total Population

| *State* | *Total Population* | *Area (Sq. kms)* | *Density (Persons/ Sq. kms)* | *SC (%)* | *ST (%)* |
|---|---|---|---|---|---|
| Arunachal Pradesh | 1097968 | 83743 | 13 | 0.56 | 64.2 |
| Assam | 26655528 | 78438 | 340 | 6.85 | 12.4 |
| Manipur | 2166788 | 22327 | 97 | 2.77 | 34.2 |
| Meghalaya | 2318822 | 22429 | 103 | 0.48 | 85.9 |
| Mizoram | 888573 | 21081 | 42 | 0.03 | 94.5 |
| Nagaland | 1990036 | 16579 | 120 | | 89.1 |
| Sikkim | 540851 | 7096 | 76 | 5.02 | 20.6 |
| Tripura | 3199203 | 10486 | 305 | 17.37 | 31.1 |
| **NER Total** | **38857769** | **262179** | **148** | **6.40** | **26.93** |
| **All India** | **1026443540** | **3166285** | **324** | **16.20** | **8.1** |

*Source*: Primary Census Abstract: Census of India 2001.

As it is given in Table 1.3, the population density of the region was 148 persons per sq. km which is less than the national average of 324. Among the NE states, Arunachal Pradesh has the lowest population density followed by Mizoram; while Assam has the highest followed by Tripura.

Mizoram, as it is given in Table 1.5 has the highest literacy rate at 88.80 per cent, which is the second in India after Kerala; while lowest literacy rate is observed in Arunachal Pradesh (54.30%), which is below the national average of 62.8 per cent. For the states of Manipur, Meghalaya, Nagaland, Sikkim, Assam and Tripura the literacy rate was in the range 60-75 per cent. In respect of female literacy, it is highest in Mizoram (86.70%) and lowest in Arunachal Pradesh; while it was in the range 54-65 per cent in all other states. The sex ratio is found to be highest in Manipur (978) and lowest in Sikkim (875). Further, according to the 2001 census, more than 70 per cent of the total population lived in rural areas in all States of NER except for Mizoram in which rural population accounted for 50.37 per cent.

**Table 1.4:** Literacy Rates and Sex Ratios in North-Eastern Region

| *State* | *Population* | | | *Literacy Rate* | | | *Sex Ratio* |
|---|---|---|---|---|---|---|---|
| | *Person* | *Male* | *Female* | *Person* | *Male* | *Female* | |
| Arunachal Pradesh | 1097968 | 579941 | 518027 | 54.30 | 63.84 | 43.54 | 893 |
| Assam | 26655528 | 13777037 | 12878491 | 63.37 | 71.30 | 54.60 | 935 |
| Manipur | 2166788 | 1095634 | 1071154 | 70.50 | 80.30 | 60.50 | 978 |
| Meghalaya | 2318822 | 1176087 | 1142735 | 62.60 | 65.40 | 59.60 | 972 |
| Mizoram | 888573 | 459109 | 429464 | 88.80 | 90.70 | 86.70 | 935 |
| Nagaland | 1990036 | 1047141 | 942895 | 66.60 | 71.20 | 61.50 | 900 |
| Sikkim | 540851 | 288484 | 252367 | 68.80 | 76.00 | 60.40 | 875 |
| Tripura | 3199203 | 1642225 | 1556978 | 73.20 | 81.00 | 64.90 | 948 |

*Source*: *Primary Census Abstract*: *Census of India 2001.*

**Table 1.5:** Distribution of Population by Area-2001 (Persons)

| *State* | *Total* | *Rural* | *Urban* | *Rural* (%) | *Urban* (%) |
|---|---|---|---|---|---|
| Arunachal Pradesh | 1097961 | 870087 | 227881 | 79.25 | 20.75 |
| Assam | 26655528 | 23216288 | 3439240 | 87.10 | 12.90 |
| Manipur | 2166700 | 1590820 | 575968 | 73.42 | 26.58 |
| Meghalaya | 2318822 | 1864711 | 454111 | 80.42 | 19.58 |
| Mizoram | 888575 | 447567 | 441006 | 50.37 | 49.63 |
| Nagaland | 1990036 | 1647249 | 342787 | 82.77 | 17.23 |
| Sikkim | 540851 | 480981 | 59870 | 88.93 | 11.07 |
| Tripura | 3199203 | 2653453 | 545750 | 82.94 | 17.06 |
| **NER Total** | **38857676** | **32771156** | **6086613** | **84.34** | **15.66** |
| **All India** | **1.029E+09** | **742490639** | **286119689** | **72.18** | **27.82** |

*Source*: *NER Basic Statistics 2006.*

### 1.10.4 The Economy

The Net State Domestic Product (NSDP) at Factor Cost and per capita NSDP at constant prices (1999-00 as base year), for all States for the year 1999-00 and 2005-06 are given in Table 1.6. The Per Capita NSDP in North-Eastern India ranged from Rs. 14786.00 in Assam to Rs. 21524 in Sikkim. For the states of Arunachal Pradesh, Manipur, Meghalaya, Mizoram, Nagaland and Tripura, the per capita NSDP was in the range Rs. 14786-21524.

**Table 1.6:** Net State Domestic Product at Factor Cost by Industry of Origin and Per Capita NSDP at 1999-2000 Prices in North-Eastern India

| *States* | *NSDP at Factor Cost by Industry Origin (Rs. Lac)* | | | *Per Capita NSDP (in Rs)* | | |
|---|---|---|---|---|---|---|
| | *1999-00* | *2004-05* | *2005-06* | *1990-00* | *2004-05* | *2005-06* |
| Arunachal Pradesh | 150380 | 224121 | 233030 | 13990 | 19336 | 18390 |
| Assam | 3201066 | 3977716 | 4214971 | 12282 | 14149 | 14786 |
| Manipur | 295411 | 407036 | 452195 | 13260 | 16482 | 17950 |
| Meghalaya | 326851 | 431755 | 449175 | 14347 | 17618 | 18459 |
| Mizoram | 140951 | 183939 | 196496 | 16443 | 18904 | 19691 |
| Nagaland | 255618 | 430420 | – | 13819 | 18147 | 18318 |
| Sikkim | 76536 | 110194 | 119121 | 14119 | 19825 | 21524 |
| Tripura | 449557 | 663924 | 719741 | 14890 | 19332 | 20609 |

*Source: Central Statistical Organisation (CSO).*

http://db.nedfi.com/content/nsdp-north-east-states

The economy of North-Eastern India is basically agrarian with low industrial activities where public expenditure is the main driving force of the economy. From the percentage distribution of NSDP in North-Eastern States, given in Table 1.7, for the year 2002-03, agriculture and allied activities remains the main component of states' incomes. Its share ranged from 23.66 per cent in Sikkim to 35.82 per cent in Arunachal Pradesh. The share of agriculture and allied activities in the NSDP was in the ranged 24-35 per cent in all other states. The contributions of industrial sector are more or less considerable in the states of Assam (15.33%), Meghalaya (8.96%) Manipur (7.68%); while it is not considerable in all other states. At the same time, the contribution of service sector is very high in all states of the region. It ranged from 49.83 per cent in Assam to

**Table 1.7:** Components of NSDP at Factor Cost by Industry of Origin at Constant Price (Base: 1993-94 = 100) for the year 2002-2003

| *Sates* | *Rs. Crore* | | | *Percentage Share* | | |
|---|---|---|---|---|---|---|
| | *Agriculture and Allied Activity* | *Industry* | *Service* | *Agriculture and Allied Activity* | *Industry* | *Service* |
| Arunachal Pradesh | 625.00 | 72.80 | 1047.00 | 35.82 | 4.17 | 60.01 |
| Assam | 11678.00 | 5139.00 | 16700.00 | 34.84 | 15.33 | 49.83 |
| Manipur | 989.10 | 248.60 | 2001.00 | 30.54 | 7.68 | 61.78 |
| Meghalaya | 1045.40 | 356.40 | 2574.00 | 26.29 | 8.96 | 64.74 |
| Mizoram | 490.90 | 43.60 | 1493.00 | 24.21 | 2.15 | 73.64 |
| Nagaland | 1484.60 | 6.90 | 2967.00 | 33.30 | 0.15 | 66.55 |
| Sikkim | 262.80 | 61.50 | 786.40 | 23.66 | 5.54 | 70.80 |
| Tripura | 1823.60 | 220.80 | 4040.00 | 29.97 | 3.63 | 66.40 |

*Source*: *Central Statistical Organisation (CSO).*
http://db.nedfi.com/content/nsdp-north-east-states

73.64 per cent in Mizoram. The major crops cultivated in North-Eastern Region are tea and rice; and the major minerals are coal, petroleum and natural gas.

## NOTES

1. Engel, Ernst (1857): *Die Production and Consumtionswerhaltnisse des Konigreichs Sachsen.* Dresden.
2. *Ducpetiaux* (1855): Budgets econoiques des classes ouvricres en Belgique, Brussel.
3. Houthakker, H.S. (1957): An International Comparison of Household Expenditure Patterns, Commemorating the Centenary of Engel's Law. *Econometrica*, Vol. 25, No. 4 (Oct.), pp. 532-551.
4. Keynes, J.M. (1936): *The General Theory of Employment, Interest and Money*. Macmillan, New York.
5. Duessenberry, James (1949): *Income, Saving and the Theory of Consumer Behaviour*. Harvard University Press, Cambridge, Massachussets, 1967.
6. *Ibid.*

7. Friedman, Milton (1957): *A Theory of Consumption Function.* Oxford & BH Publishing Co. New Delhi, 1970.
8. Modigliani, Franco and Richard Brumberg (1963): *Utility Analysis and Consumption Function: An Interpretation of Cross section data.* Post Keynesian Economics, Rutgers Univ. Press. pp. 388-436; and Modigliani, F. and A. Ando: The Life Cycle Hypothesis of Saving: Aggregate Implications and Tests. *American Economic Review*, Vol. 53, (1963) pp. 56-83.
9. *Ibid.*
10. Farrel, M.J. (1959): *The New Theories of Consumption Function.* Economic Journal Vol. 69, pp. 678-696.

## REFERENCES


1. Stigler, George J. (1954): The Early History of Empirical Studies of Consumer Behaviour. *The Journal of Political Economy*, Vol. LXII, April, pp. 95-113.
2. Upender, M. (1998): Estimates of Expenditure Elasticities of Demand. *Finance India*, Vol. XII, No. 3, September.
3. Sinha, R.P. (1966): An Analysis of Food Expenditure in India. *Journal of Farm Economics*, Vol. 48, No. 1 (Feb.), pp. 113-123.
4. Gupta, D.B. (1968): A Comparison of Consumption Patterns in Uttar Pradesh and Madras—A study of inter-regional variations with reference to India. *Indian Economic Review*, New Series, 3, pp. 129-144
5. Prasad, A.R. (2001): *Consumption Behaviour in India: Theory and Evidence.* Reliance Publishing House, New Delhi pp. 342-343.
6. Rudra, A. (1972): *Survey of Research on Consumption, Saving sand Capital Formation.* The Data Base of Indian Economy. Indian Econometric Society, New Delhi.
7. Rudra, A. (1976): Consumption, Savings and Capital Formation—A Trend Report, in Lakdawala, D.T. (ed.), *A Survey of Research in Economics, Vol. 2, Macro-economics*, (ICSSR Project), Allied Publishers, New Delhi, pp. 47-123.
8. Samuelson, P.A.: The Simple Mathematics of Income Determination, in *Income, Employment, and Public Policy* (W.W. Norton, 1948), Reprinted in W.L. Johnson and D.R. Kamerschen (Eds.), *Macroeconomics: Selected Readings* (Houghton Miffin 1970), pp. 39-49.

9. North-Eastern Council (2006): *Basic Statistics of North Eastern Region.* Ministry of Home Affairs, Govt. of India.
10. Ackley, G. (1969): *Macroeconomic Theory.* MacMillan Company, New York.
11. Koutsoyannis, A. (1979): *Modern Microeconomics.* 2nd ed. McMillan, Hongkong.

# 2
# Review of Literature

The literature on the study of consumer behaviour can be broadly classified into three, namely, study based on family budget data, demand analysis and consumption functions. Study on family budget data relates to the changes in consumption of particular consumption items to a change in income and estimation of expenditure elasticities of demand for that consumption items. Secondly, studies on the demand theory relates to the fitting of functional relationship between quantity demand and price and estimation of price elasticities of demand. Finally, the consumption function relates to the study on the determinants of aggregate consumption and the estimation of marginal propensity to consume.

Since the study of consumption patterns is primarily the study of family budget data and its allocation to the consumption of various consumption items, and the estimation of consumption function, the present book concentrates on (i) the study of family budget data and its allocation to various items of consumption goods, and (ii) estimation of aggregate consumption function. Various economists study the consumption by fitting Engel's curve and estimating the expenditure elasticities of demand for various commodities to the changes in total incomes of the families and estimated the propensities to consume by fitting consumption function. Most of the studies analyzed the consumption patterns by estimating various forms of Engel's functions, viz, linear function, double-logarithmic function, semi-logarithmic function, log-log-inverse function. At the same time, analyses of the effects of household size on consumption and the existence of economies of scale in consumptions have also been made in some studies.

An outlines of some of the literatures related to the study of consumption patterns have been given in the present chapters. They are divided, in this chapter, into two broad areas studies based on households expenditure on various items of consumption and aggregate consumption, each is sub-divided into two viz, global studies on consumption patterns and studies of consumption patterns in India.

## 2.1 PATTERN OF HOUSEHOLD CONSUMPTION EXPENDITURE ON ITEMS OF CONSUMPTION

### 2.1.1 Brief Review of Global Studies

The study of consumption behaviour occupied one of the most important fields of research in economics since 1857 when Engel published his law of consumption called 'Engel's Law'. Since then, studies on consumption behaviour increased enormously in volume and improved substantially in quality. The budget studies made by Ducpetiaux (1855)[1] in the economy of Saxony and Prussia for the year of 1848 and 1855 respectively were perhaps the first empirical analysis of family budgets collection and classification of expenditure data among various commodities. He collected almost 200 families' budgets and published in his book the distribution of expenditure among various commodity groups. This was followed with the popularization of statistical analysis of social and economic data.

The first and most famous statistical analysis of budget was made by Ernst Engel in 1857. Engel's analysis rested on the data collected by Ducpetiaux (1855)[2] from 153 Belgian families which had been classified into three social-economic groups: families dependent upon public assistance, families just able to live without such assistance and families in comfortable circumstances. On the basis of this study, Engel proposed a law of consumption, which was then known to be the famous 'Engel's Law'. Engel's Law states the proportion of income spent on food declines as income increases. 'The poorer a family, the greater the proportion of its total expenditure, that must be devoted to the provision of food' (Engel, 1857)[3]. He also made further analysis of Ducpetiaux's data in 1895 by income class rather than by socio-economic classes and proved the validity of his earlier law of consumption.

Schwabe (1868)[4] proposed that the poorer anyone is, the greater the amount relative to his income that he must spend for housing. Wright (1875)[5] in his study confirmed Engel's law and Schwabe's law and reiterated the law of consumer behaviour. His law stated that the higher the income, the greater the saving actually and proportionately. Vecchio (1912)[6] calculated expenditure elasticity of food by estimating a semi-logarithmic function where consumption expenditure was used as dependent variable and log of the total expenditure (or income) was used as an explanatory variable. He found that the proportion of income spent on food decreases as income increases as proposed by Engel in his Law of Consumption.

A number of studies had been made on consumption patterns based on family budget data since the later part of the 19th century. However, there were no systematic studies on households' budgets until 1930's (Stigler, 1954)[7]. Various economists had started to study households' consumer expenditure using various statistical and econometrics tools since 1930's.

Leser (1941)[8] calculated the income elasticity of demand for various commodity groups using linear Engel function based on the cost of living studies for 12,096 white families in 92 cities in USA for the period of 1918-19. In his study he assumed that total expenditure equals income and accordingly he used total expenditure instead of total income as an independent variable in the Engel Function. He found that four commodity groups: (i) food; (ii) Housing; (iii) fuel, light and refrigeration; and (iv) tobacco have an inelastic demand with regard to income (i.e. expenditure elasticities are less than one). Other five groups: (1) transportation; (2) other household operations; (3) recreation; (4) clothing; and (5) miscellaneous, which have the highest income elasticities, have at the same time a price elastic demand.

Burk (1951)[9], based on the data of US Department of Commerce, analyzed the changing pattern of food consumption in between 1941 and 1950. He made comparison of the actual expenditure pattern during the period of 1941 to 1950 with the estimated expenditure pattern on the basis of the Engel's function calculated by him using the data covering 1929 to 1941. He observed that:

(1) on the basis of changes in average income and in the distribution of income, but there is no change in income-elasticity of demand (i.e. 0.8), food expenditures was expected to take 24 per cent of income in 1948, and about the same proportion in the following two years; and
(2) use of postwar average incomes per capita with the pattern of relationships of food expenditures to disposable income in prewar years 1929-41 indicates that food expenditures in 1947 were roughly 25 per cent higher than expected: 20 per cent in 1948, 15 per cent in 1949; but it was only about 10 per cent in 1950.

His observations of gradual reduction in the gap between actual and estimated food expenditures led him to make the hypothesis that the relatively high levels of food expenditures in 1946-48 may have been temporary. He pointed out two obvious factors:

(1) the natural lag in adjustment of food consumption pattern to rapid postwar changes in income and to the relative scarcity of supplies and price rise of food and nonfood commodities; and
(2) the availability of unusual sources of purchasing power over and above the current income during the postwar period.

Houthakker (1957)[10] commemorating the centenary of Engel's law made an international comparison of household expenditures. Elasticities for food, clothing, housing and miscellaneous items with respect to total expenditures and family size were being compared based on regression analysis of 40 surveys from 35 countries. Interestingly, the elasticities are found to be more or less similar in these countries. He used the model of the form

$$\log y_i = \alpha_i + \beta \log X_i + g_i \log X_2 + e_i \qquad \text{... (2.1)}$$

where $Y_i$ is expenditure on the ith group of items, $X_1$ is total expenditure, $X_2$ is family size, $e_i$ is a disturbance term, and $\alpha$, $\beta$ and $\gamma$ are constant to be estimated. After estimating the Engel's curve for these countries he found that

(1) the elasticities of expenditure for food are all significantly less than one and therefore confirm Engel's law. The highest figure being 0.731 for Poland and the lowest 0.344 for the middle class survey of United Kingdoms;
(2) the elasticities for clothing with respect to total expenditure are all greater than unity. As such, clothing can be considered as luxury items;
(3) the elasticities for housing are mostly below one. Hence housing can be considered as necessity. It was found that these elasticities are smallest among the larger cities especially in UK and USA;
(4) the elasticities for miscellaneous expenditures are well above one;
(5) elasticities for food with respect to family size are all significantly positive, and mostly between 0.2 and 0.35. Interestingly, he found that in most of these countries where $\beta$'s are large, $\gamma$'s tend to be smaller; and
(6) the partial elasticities for food with respect to family size are all significantly positive, and mostly between 0.2 and 0.35.

Leser (1963)[11] tried the various forms of Engel functions and made critical examinations of their appropriateness to be a generally accepted form. He selected five functional forms, which were used by economists to examine the pattern of consumer expenditures. Leser selected the following functional forms:

$$w_i = \alpha_i + \beta_i M + \varepsilon_i \quad \text{... (2.2)}$$
$$v_i = \alpha_i + \beta_i M + \varepsilon_i \quad \text{... (2.3)}$$
$$w_i = \alpha_i + \beta_i / M + \varepsilon_i \quad \text{... (2.4)}$$
$$\log w_i = \alpha_i + \beta_i \log M + \varepsilon_i \quad \text{... (2.5)}$$
$$w_i = \alpha_i + \beta_i \log M + \varepsilon_i \quad \text{... (2.6)}$$

where M is income, $v_i$ is total expenditure on commodity group *i* and $w_i = v_i/M$.

He tested the relative usefulness of each functional form on the data of family expenditure and income of Ireland during 1950-51. Ten commodity groups were selected for examination. It was found that coefficient of determination ($R^2$) differ from one another for each of the commodity group. Accordingly, the estimated income elasticity differs for each of the functional form. Thus, any single functional forms did not satisfy all the requirements—both a priori and statistical criteria—for all commodities. This necessitates the proper choice of the functional form for different items.

He used the estimated parameters in the different models to calculate the average income elasticity of marginal outlays using the following formula

$$\gamma(G) = \frac{b_i}{a_i + b_i(1 + \log G)}$$

where $G = M$.

He found that the average income elasticity of marginal outlays as follows:

(1) –0.27 for food and beverages,
(2) –1.21 for tobacco,
(3) 1.36 for dwelling,
(4) –0.20 for house furnishings and equipment,
(5) –0.16 for clothing,
(6) –0.20 for fuel, light, etc.,
(7) 0.13 for transportation,
(8) 0.13 for medical care, and
(9) 0.77 for miscellaneous.

Nisbet and Vakil (1972)[12] made an estimate of price elasticity of demand for marijuana among the students of University of California and Los Angeles' (UCLA). The study was based on the data collected through anonymous mail questionnaire covering 926 respondents. They used double-log and linear function to estimate elasticities in which prices of marijuana and total monthly expenditures are used as independent variables. For both functional forms only price was statistically significant explanatory variables for the consumption of marijuana. The estimates of price elasticities of demand around the market prices ranged from –0.40 to –0.51 depending on the type of data used and on the functional forms. On the other hand, the estimated expenditure elasticities are not significantly different from zero. This study suggests that an individual's consumption of marijuana depends on factors other than total expenditures.

With the objectives of testing the validity of testing Engel's law Nadeem and Khan (1991)[13] examined the household consumption patterns separately for the urban and the rural sectors in Pakistan by estimating the marginal expenditure shares and expenditure elasticities, for twelve broad commodity groups, using the micro level data of the Household Income and Expenditure Survey (HIES) for the year 1984-85, compiled by the Statistics Division of the Government of Pakistan. This survey, based on a national sample, covered 16580 households. Various commodities, in this study, have been grouped into twelve major categories, namely, Food and Drinks, Clothing and Footwear, Fuel and Lighting, Housing, Transport and Communications, Household Effects, Personal Effects, Health Care, Education, Entertainment, Durables, and Miscellaneous items.

In this study, both linear and double-logarithmic functional forms of the Engel's curve are estimated with the help of the Ordinary Least Square (OLS) method. The results reported in the paper indicate that there is not much difference between the estimates obtained with the 'community effects' and those obtained without it. The results of the studies indicated that as the level of income increases, the share of Food and Drinks in total household expenditure declines for households in both the urban and the rural sectors. They claimed their finding was completely in conformity with Engel's law. The expenditure share of Transport and Communication was found to rise with the level of income, while that of Clothing and Footwear and Fuel and Lighting declines in the case of rural households. The results further indicated that the expenditure elasticity of Food and Drinks was less than unity in both the urban and the rural sectors as well as for households in different income groups within each sector. Furthermore, it has a tendency to decline with the level of income. The expenditure elasticities of other commodities not only vary widely across different income groups within each sector, but they also exhibited a cyclical pattern. The expenditure elasticities of different commodities with respect to the household-size confirm the existence of economies of scale in the consumption of a majority of the commodities considered in this paper. The results further suggest that the degrees of economies of scale not only differ across commodities but are also different across sectors, as well as across different income groups within each sector. Finally, the results of this study indicated that the observed differences in the consumption patterns of the urban and the rural households represent structural as well as behavioural differences.

An Economic Research Service (1997)[14], US Department of Agriculture, in its analysis of 51 countries observed that on average, high-income countries spend 16 per cent of their expenditures on food, while low-income countries spend 55 per cent. It was further observed in the study that rising income levels generally result in a more diverse diet and, hence the composition of food demand will undergo a greater change in developing countries compared with developed countries.

Regmi, *et al.* (2001)[15] used the data of International Comparison Project (IPC), Statistical Advisory Services of World Bank, for the year of 1996 to analyze the food consumption pattern of 115 countries ranging from low-income to high-income countries. The data covered expenditures and price data for 10 broad consumption categories and 22 sub-categories. Their analysis employed a two-stage budgeting process which assumes that consumers first allocate their budget to broad consumption groups. Accordingly, they first estimated an aggregate demand system across 10 broad consumption categories. The second stage of the analysis involved the estimation of parameters for the sub-categories of food items. To estimate the parameters they used the Working's Preference Independence Model and Working Slutsky Model developed by Theil, Chung and Scale (1989)[16] for the first stage and the second stages respectively.

They found that, on the average, low-income countries spend a greater portion of their budget on food and are more responsive to income and food price than middle and high-income countries. They observed that:

(1) for all food sub-groups, poorer countries exhibit a greater responsiveness to changes in income levels,
(2) the demand for staple food, such as cereals, fats and oils, fruits and vegetables, is less responsive to income changes,
(3) food sub-group price change responsiveness was independent on income levels, and

(4) cereals price changes inversely affect the demand for fruit and vegetables.

This paper provides further evidence that both the budget share allocated to food, as well as the income elasticity of food decline as income increases. And low-value staples, such as cereals, account for a larger share of the food budget in poorer countries, while high-value food items such as dairy and meat are a larger share of the food budget in richer countries.

Lanfranco, *et al.* (2000)[17] studied the food elasticities of demand of the US's Hispanic community from the cross-sectional data sets collected from 673 Hispanic households by USDA in its Continuing Survey of Food Intakes by Individuals. They used semi-logarithmic model to estimate Engel curves. They found, on the average, the demand for particular food groups appears to be relatively inelastic with respect to income, and moderately to unitary elastic with respect to household size. They claimed that the result they had found were consistent with demand studies previously undertaken for the whole US population, and suggest that Engel's law holds for individual food categories with regard to Hispanic consumers in the US.

Chern, *et al.* (2002)[18], based on the Annual Report on the Family Income and Expenditure Survey in 1997 by Statistical Bureau, Management and Coordination Agency of Japan, and they made an analysis on the food consumption patterns and made an econometric analysis of food demand structure in Japan. The study covered 11 major food items, and the total number of observations used for estimation was 95,223. Various single equation models: Working-Leser model, Tobit Model, Linearly Approximated Almost Ideal Demand System and non-linear Almost Ideal Demand System were applied in this study.

They found from the 11 major food items, the expenditure elasticity of rice is positive and close to one. The result proves that rice consumed in Japan is normal good, contrary to the results from the preceding studies. Marshallian uncompensated and Hicksian compensated own-price elasticities for rice are highly elastic in all models; on the other hand, the own price elasticity for meat is relatively price inelastic. Fresh meats and rice are mild complements in all models; however, fresh fish and rice show the mixed results with respect to their substitution pattern. Further, according to their meat demand analysis it was concluded that Japanese dietary patterns have become more and more westernized.

The Provincial Decision-Making Enabling (PROVIDE) Project (2003)[19] examined the impact of income levels in determining household expenditure patterns and the effects of location (rural/urban) on household consumption patterns in South Africa based on the Income and Expenditure Survey (IES), Central Statistics Services, South Africa, data for the year 1995. It was found that the level of household income is often a major determinant of expenditure patterns of households, and hence differences between patterns of expenditure are largely a reflection of differences in income between household groups or individual households. However, income is not the only determinant and various factors, most importantly race and location, also affect preferences and hence expenditure patterns.

Burger, *et al.* (2004)[20] made a comparison to the living standards and consumption patterns of black households to those of a representative South African sample in an attempt to better understand the phenomenon of the rising black middle class. They used the data of Income and Expenditure Survey of South Africa for the year 2000. By fitting the double-log engel curves, they observed that the consumption patterns in South Africa are largely in agreement with international evidence which confirmed engel law for (by Houthakker, 1957 and Leser, 1963). Comparison of the consumption patterns of black households with full sample of households to examine racial differences in spending patterns revealed that despite the close match in average expenditure, the top black quintiles' spending patterns differ markedly from the consumption behaviour of Indian and coloured households and diverge even further from white consumption patterns.

Kushwaha, *et al.* (2007)[21] examined the household consumption of vegetable products in the rural and urban areas of Kano state of Nigeria. Data were collected from sixty (60) randomly selected households in both rural and urban areas using cluster random sampling techniques. The data collection was achieved through the use of structured questionnaires. The data were analyzed using descriptive statistics, correlation and estimation of various forms of Engel's curves, viz, linear, semi-log, and double-log, by OLS.

The results of the study revealed that, the quantity of vegetables consumed in the rural area recorded a minimum of 129.65 grams per household per week with a maximum of 769.95 grams per household per week. An average quantity consumed was 451.08 gram per household per week with a standard error of 0.28 and a coefficient of variability was 3.91%. Whereas, the quantity of vegetables consumed in the urban study area had a minimum of 603.65 gram per household per week with a maximum of 4156.00 grams per household per week. The average quantity consumed was 1781.78 grams per household per week, with a standard error of 0.832 and a coefficient of variability of 3.6%. Socio economic factors showed little influence on consumption compared with economic parameters.

The analysis shows that the quantity consumed per household in the study area is positively correlated with the household socio-demographic parameters as well as all the economic variables. It however, indicates a negative relationship with the status of house wife showing that, the more highly placed a housewife is the lesser her level of utilization of the vegetable products. Similar relationship exists between years of formal education of the household head and consumption of the vegetable products. They also found some positive significant relationship at ($p<0.05$) between adult and form of utilization, expenditure on food and expenditure on vegetable disposable income for consumer in Kano State. It was also found that, income was the most important factors affecting vegetable consumption pattern in urban areas unlike in the rural, and that the higher income earners (urban consumers) spend more proportion of their earning on food than lower income group.

### 2.1.2 Brief Review of Studies in India

Not much work was done in the field of statistical studies on consumer behaviour in India before 1950, although the budget studies were being carried out in small areas. The situation changed rapidly when demand projections were needed in connection with the formulation of the Second Five Year Plan side by side with the starting of the collection of households' budget data by NSS since 1950. So the first country estimates of demand elasticities with repect to per capita household consumer expenditure were computed by Roy and Laha[22] in 1954 using NSS data. Since then a large number of studies in India have been carried out by many workers, mostly on the basis of NSS data.

Iyengar (1960)[23] calculated Engel elasticities for some commodity groups using the Consumer Expenditure Data of India for 1955-56. In stead of estimating Engel's curve to find expenditure elasticities, he estimated Engel's expenditure elasticities using (a) Lorenz curve which relates the proportion of total expenditure to the proportion of persons spending up to a given level of total expenditure per capita, and (b) the specific concentration curve which relates the proportion of total consumption of a specific concentration commodity to the proportion of persons spending up to a given level of total expenditure per capita.

He found in his study that the commodities which have higher concentration ratios have high expenditure elasticities. He observed that health care, which has the highest concentration ratio (0.64), has the highest expenditure elasticity. It is also found in his study that commodity group of food has less than unity elasticity (i.e. food is necessity) while clothing, milk and milk products, and health has more than unity elasticities (i.e. these commodity groups are luxury). However, his method was not applicable in cases where the concentration curves are not symmetric. The method used by him was rather complicated.

Sinha (1966)[24] estimated the elasticities of expenditures on various items of food in India based on the cross-sectional data of various rounds of National Sample Surveys in 1950's. For lack of published data, he used total expenditure per person as principal explanatory variable while fitting Engel's curve rather than income. To calculate expenditure elasticities he fitted eight forms of Engel's curve, namely, linear, double-log, semi-log, log-inverse, log-log-inverse and hyperbolic curves. He found that log-log-inverse function gave the highest values of $R^2$ in rural areas for total food, food grains, milk products, meat, fish, and eggs, sugar, and other foods. In case of urban samples, it gave the highest value of $R^2$ for total food, milk products, edible oil, meat, fish and eggs, and sugar only. He concluded, base on the test of goodness of fit and no autocorrelation, that no single regression form was suitable for all items of food.

He also elaborated the regional variations of food consumption behaviour among various regions of the country. For India as a whole, expenditure elasticities for food-grains, milk and milk products, edible oil, sugar, and salt are higher in rural areas than in urban areas. As against this, the elasticities for meat, fish, and eggs, for the miscellaneous food groups, and for total food are higher for the urban areas. He pointed out two main reasons for these differences: (a) average income per person is higher in urban areas, and (b) with growing urbanization, there is a normal tendency towards diversification of food and towards an increase in expenditure on food taken outside one's home.

He further, elaborated the differences in the consumptions of some commodity groups among the regions of the country. Based on the rural samples it had been found that

(1) the highest expenditure elasticities for food grains occurred in the South and the lowest in the Western part of the country,
(2) milk products have elasticities of more than unity in all the region—Eastern region being the highest and Western region the lowest, and

(3) expenditure elasticities of sugar are more than unity in all the regions except for Northern region.

In case of urban samples, on the other hand, it was observed that:

(1) elasticity of total food expenditure is the lowest in the South and the highest in the West,
(2) East has the highest elasticity for milk products,
(3) edible oil has the lowest elasticity in the North West and the West has the highest, and
(4) for sugar, the elasticity is slightly more than one only for the North and East and is very close to unity for the Central area.

Further, he observed estimates of elasticities for the various rounds of the NSS showed considerable variation. He believed such variations were caused by sampling fluctuations, changes in income in different seasons, the seasonal variations in relative prices, and the availability of the different items of food in different seasons.

Iyengar, *et al.* (1968)[25], examining the effect of household size on consumption pattern, fitted Engel's function of the form

$$\log y = \alpha + \beta \log x + \gamma \log n \qquad \text{... (2.7)}$$

where $\beta$ and $\gamma$ are the elasticities of consumption with respect to total consumer expenditure and household size and $\beta + \gamma$ measures the degree of economies of scale in consumption. They used ungrouped NSS 17th round budget data for two states, Madras and Uttar Pradesh, and selected the following items for analysis: total cereals, milk and milk products, fuel and light, and clothing. The analysis was carried out separately for rural and urban sectors of the states. It was found that economies of scale were clear in case of cereals and fuel and light in UP as well as in Madras, but not so clear for milk and milk products or clothing, which are usually considered to be luxuries in India. The estimate of $\gamma$ was significantly positive for cereals, and fuel and light, but negative for the remaining items.

Gupta (1968)[26] also compared the consumption pattern of UP and Madras, separately for rural and urban sectors, using NSS 17th round ungrouped data on some broad item-groups as well as some detailed items of consumption. Regression equation of the form were fitted by weighted

$$\log y = \alpha + \beta \log x + \gamma \log n \qquad \text{... (2.8)}$$

least squares. Here n denotes household size and y and x, household expenditure on the particular item and total expenditure respectively. He tested the equality of state-wise regression for each sector. The between states variation was significant for many items in either sector. He also observed the significant difference within each state.

Maitra (1969)[27] examined the grouped state-wise estimates for cereals and cereals substitutes for rural India obtained from NSS rounds 13, 15, 16, 17 and 18 and also the estimates of quantitative consumption of rice, wheat and total cereals based on the 17th round. The log-log inverse and semi-log forms of the engel curve, especially the former, were found to provide the best fit to the data. Analysis of covariance tests showed the marked variation in the elasticities over different states for a given round, while the variation in the elasticities over rounds for a particular state to be less pronounced.

Bhattacharya and Maitra (1969)[28] carried out an extensive analysis of engel curves using grouped NSS data for rural and urban India for 14 or 15 broad commodity groups. Data for 14th round to the 22nd round of NSS were covered in the analysis. Four algebraic forms, viz, hyperbolic, semi-log, double-log and log-log-inverse were compared on the basis of measures of goodness of fit like coefficient of determination ($R^2$) and measures of randomness like the Durbin-Watson statistic (d). The log-log-inverse was found to be generally satisfactory and provided the best fit in most cases. The residuals from this curve were nearly random, unlike those from other forms. The semi-log and double-log were sometimes nearly as good, but the hyperbola was acceptable for cereals and substitutes and pulses in the urban sector. The relative standing of semi-log and double-log depend to some extent on whether one directly compares the $R^2$ for the two curves. Singh (1973)[29] also compared the $\overline{R}^2$ for ten algebraic forms in course of his investigation of the effects of household composition on consumption patterns. He observed that the parabola, log-log-inverse and semi-log-inverse were the most successful and the straight line and the double-log were quite poor. However, it should be noted that the sample sizes were quite small in this study.

Coondoo (1969)[30] examined how far inter-temporal movements of Engel elasticity for cereal consumption in India depend upon the price of cereals relative to the general price level as also on the relative prices of the items constituting the cereals group. He used the time series data on consumer expenditure by NSS rounds from the 4th through the 18th both for rural and urban areas. To examine the influence of the relative prices of cereals as a group he tried double logarithmic relationship of the following forms for rural and urban India separately.

$$\log \eta_{vi} = \alpha + \beta \log \left( \frac{p}{\overline{p}} \right)_t + \varepsilon_t \qquad \ldots (2.9)$$

And

$$\log \eta_{vi} = \alpha + \beta \log \left( \frac{p}{\overline{p}} \right)_t + \gamma \log \left( \frac{p_s}{p_i} \right)_t + \varepsilon_t \qquad \ldots (2.10)$$

Where

$\eta_{vi}$ : Engel's elasticity for value of cereals consumed in round t.

$\left( \frac{p}{\overline{p}} \right)_t$ : Ratio of cereal price and general price in the form of an index for round t

$\left( \frac{p_s}{p_i} \right)_t$ : Ratio of prices of superior and inferior cereals in round t, where 's' stands for superior cereals which include rice and wheat, and 'i' stands for inferior cereals group represented by jowar and ragi.

The estimated equations suggested $\left( \frac{p}{\overline{p}} \right)$ as a major determinant of value of elasticity in rural India. In all the equations for rural India the coefficients of $\left( \frac{p}{\overline{p}} \right)$, whether wholesale or retail, turned out to be significant. On the other hand, $\left( \frac{p_s}{p_i} \right)$ fails to show any significant influence on value elasticity even for rural India. For urban India the standard errors of all estimated coefficients were high and as a result the influence of $\left( \frac{p}{\overline{p}} \right)$ or $\left( \frac{p_s}{p_i} \right)$ on $\eta_{vi}$ were not at all evident. In view of these result, he concluded that there is considerable evidence of the inter-relatedness of $\eta_{vi}$, the engel elasticity, and $\left( \frac{p}{\overline{p}} \right)$, the relative price of cereals as a group, at least for rural India.

Singh and Singh (1971)[31] examined expenditure patterns in Punjab utilizing the data of various rounds of National Sample Survey covering the period of 1961-62, 1964-65 and 1967-68. They examined the concentrations in consumer expenditure and estimated the expenditure elasticities for 15 commodity groups. Linear, semi-logarithmic and double-log Engel functions were being used in the study where the total expenditure for all items was used as explanatory variable. They observed that more than half of the population in the lower expenditure groups in the rural areas accounts for about one-third of the total consumer expenditure. The upper 15 per cent of the population incurs nearly 30 per cent of the total consumer expenditure. In the urban areas also more than half of the poorest population accounts for about one-third of the total consumer expenditure. But the richest 14 per cent of the population incurs about 30 per cent of the total consumer expenditure in urban areas.

In respect of expenditure elasticities of demand, the study found that the expenditure elasticity of demand for food items was found to be low both for rural and urban areas; while the expenditure elasticity for non-food item was found to be quite high for both rural and urban areas. Within the food group, the elasticities for cereals, pulses, milk and milk products, and salt and spices were found to be low—the magnitudes were found to be slightly higher in rural areas than in urban areas. The elasticities for meat, egg and fish, and sugar were found to be high in both rural and urban areas. Further, the expenditure elasticities for pan, tobacco and intoxicants, fuel and lighting, clothing, and durable goods have been found to be quite high both in the urban and rural areas.

Jain and Tendulkar (1972)[32] investigated occupational differences in the pattern of consumer expenditure. NSS 19th Round data for rural and urban India were used for this purpose. The ten major occupation divisions were merged to get five groups, viz., (1) divisions 0, 1 and 2, (2) division 3, (3) division 4, (4) division 7-8, and (5) divisions 0, 1 and 2. Group 1 and 2 cover the white collar occupations; group 4 and 5 the blue collar one, while the third group covers agricultural occupations. After some general examination of the estimates of average household size etc, the authors fitted engel curves for each of 9 selected items

$$y = \alpha^{(k)} + \beta^{(k)}x \qquad \ldots (2.11)$$

Where $k$ denotes the occupation group, and $x$ and $y$ have their usual significance. These equations were fitted by weighted least squares to the averages of $x$ and $y$ for 13 size classes of $x$.

Analysis of covariance tests were applied for examining the

homogeneity of the engel curves for the 5 occupation groups. In 12 out of the 18 cases, the hypothesis of homogeneity was rejected, and these cases included food grains, milk and milk products and clothing in both the sectors. The hypothesis of equality of the $\beta$'s was rejected in 13 cases including those mentioned above. The authors also carried out pair-wise comparisons between the occupational groups to locate the pairs of groups differing significantly in respect of the consumption pattern. On the whole, in the rural sector, occupation groups 4 and 5 appeared to be similar to the third group, but groups 1 and 2 were different in many respects. In the urban sector, occupation differences seemed to be greater.

Coondoo (1975)[33] made a comparison of consumer expenditure patterns of Indian middle class and working class households, residing at each of four selected urban centers, viz., Admednabad, Kanpur, Calcutta and Madras. He collected data from the published reports on the Family Living Surveys of 1958-59 and unpublished tabulations available at the Indian Statistical Institutes. He used double-log and log-log-inverse Engel's curves to asses the expenditure elasticities for the two classes. Analysis of covariance tests was applied to test the homogeneity of Engel's functions for the two social classes at each centre.

Analysis of Covariance at different centre showed similar expenditure patterns for the two social classes. It was also observed that the different centres did not show a significant differences in consumption patterns, i.e. engel elasticities for different items were similar at all the centres. For the middle class families, inter-regional homogeneity of expenditure pattern was established only for cereals and pulses. For working class families, expenditure patterns for fuel and light were also similar. In all other cases the engel functions differed as a result of significant differences in the intercepts only. For working class families, the expenditure patterns for pan, supari and tobacco and miscellaneous non-food items showed significant regional homogeneity. In addition to this, it was further observed that working class households spent higher proportions of their budget on food items compared with middle class households at the same level of per capita consumer expenditure.

Coondoo, *et al.* (1981)[34] attempted to focus attention on the role of non-monetized consumption in the empirical analysis of consumer behaviour based on the data of 18th NSS Round. They argued that the usual Engel curve analysis might not be adequate in a predominantly rural agricultural economy like India where the extent of non-monetized consumption is considerably high. In such a situation the theoretical model of consumer behaviour needs to be spelt out and proper treatment of non-monetized consumption should also be made in empirical analysis. Separate regressions for the usual Engel curve, cash consumption and kind (quantity) consumption were estimated using Double-Log function. It was observed from their result that consumption of a particular item groups are less responsive to variation in total cash consumption than total kind (quantity) consumption. So, their result suggested proper break-up of the total consumer expenditure into cash and kind should be made to estimate the Engel's curve for the economy, which is dominated by agricultural rural economy.

Upender (1998)[35] estimated the expenditure elasticities in India for 17 commodity groups based on the consumption expenditures data of the National Account Statistics for the years 1950-51 to 1993-94. The population statistic had been collected from Economic Surveys for the corresponding years and time series data at 1980-81 prices had been used to adjust the changes in prices. In order to estimate the expenditure elasticities for different item groups, he used the constant elasticity form equation,

$$\log (c/p) = a + b \log (e/p) \qquad \ldots (2.12)$$

where $c/p$ is per capita real consumption expenditure on ith item group, $e/p$ is the per capita real total expenditure and b is the expenditure elasticity.

The expenditure elasticity for food items was less than unity; and, on the other hand, it was more than unity for the group of clothing. These two findings conform to Engel's law. In case of hotels and restaurants, furniture, medical and health care, transport, education; the elasticities were all found to be higher than unity. Thus, these groups for the prevailing income level can be considered as luxury items. Interestingly, aversion behaviour has been observed towards consumption expenditures on beverages, pan, intoxicants and tobacco and its products for these groups have negative expenditure elasticities of demand.

Upender (1999)[36] made further analysis of expenditure elasticity for clothing in India using time series data from 1950-51 to 1993-94 of National Account Statistics. Engel's curves had been estimated by OLS for seven functional forms namely, linear, quadratic, semi-log, double-log, inverse, log-inverse and log-log inverse functions. It is observed from his result that the numerical values of expenditure elasticities are greater than two for all equations. This functional fit established that the proportion of total expenditure incurred on clothing increases with the increase in total expenditure. He argued that clothing has become more and more expensive among the households whose per capita incomes are very low. He pointed out three possible reasons for these phenomena that (1) rising prices of clothing, (2) falling real incomes of low-income households due to rising prices and limited incomes, and (3) demonstration effects.

Prasad (2001)[37] studied the consumption patterns in India using the time series data from 1950-51 to 1996-97. The study was based on the Central Statistical Organization (CSO) estimates of private final consumption expenditure in the domestic market taking into account the broad groups of items of consumption expenditure and their related annual aggregates published in various issues of National Account Statistics. He estimated the two types of Engel's function for all consumption items, namely, linear and double-log function and estimated the expenditure elasticities for all groups of items.

He observed that the percentage share of food expenditure in total per capita private final consumption expenditure shows a declining trend over the entire period of his study and food takes somewhat more than half of the total expenditure in India. His finding of the elasticity of food items which was as low as 0.49 proved that food is a consumption item belonging to a class of necessity. So far as the non-food expenditure is concerned, the overall expenditure elasticity turned out to be greater than one and hence the proportion of expenditure incurred on non-food items increased with an increase in total consumer expenditure.

On the basis of the estimated Engel's curves, he concluded that within non-food items, pan and tobacco are inferior commodities having less than one elasticities; while hotels, clothing, footwear, furniture, medicine, transport, recreation, education and miscellaneous are normal goods which have more than unitary elasticities. As such they can be classified as luxury items. He also found that the elasticities for beverages, rent, fuel and power were less than unity, implying that these groups of commodities are normal goods and were necessities of life. Most foods and fuels are normal goods. The elasticity of tobacco was found to be negative and is inferior commodity.

Gangopadhyay, *et al.* (2004)[38] made an exercise to: (i) derive the empirical distributions of consumption in India over the four time points, 1983, 1987-88, 1993-94 and 1999-00 using NSS data and National Account Statistics, (ii) construct the proportions of expenditure on various commodity groups, by sector and state for the different years, and (iii) calculate the NSS estimates of total expenditure for each of the commodity groups and compare them to what is reported in the National Account Statistics (NAS).

They found that over the years, there has been a growing divergence between the NSS estimates of total household consumption and the actual private consumption reported by the national accounts. Further, the extent of divergence is different for the different commodity groups. Secondly, the proportion of poor people has been declining in India. This has been brought about by a general improvement in the per capita total consumption expenditure across the country. Finally, they suggested from their empirical analysis that, a general growth in expenditure is sufficient to rid the country of poverty. Suggestion had also been made to improve the availability of those services that improve the quality of life like roads, hospitals, schooling, telecommunication and transport.

Various literature discussed so far do not give attention to the effect of reference period on Engel elasticitics of demand and studies on such effect is not very common in economic literature. Ghose and Bhattacharya (1995)[39] conducted a study on the effect of reference period on Engel elasticities of clothing and other items based on various rounds of NSS household budget data. It was observed that Engel expenditure elasticity changes dramatically for clothing with a switch in the reference period. Both in the urban and rural sectors the elasticity ranges from 2.0 to 2.2 when 'last month' data is used for clothing; but it drops to about 1.0 to 1.1 when 'annual' data is used. For durable goods, the elasticity is around 2.75 for rural India but ranges from 2.6 to 3.2 for urban areas with data relate to the 'last month'; but it drops to about 2.1 to 2.2 for both the sectors when 'annual data' is used. Thus, it may be concluded that the Engel elasticities depend critically on the reference period, which, at the same time, suggested the temporal character of household consumption behaviour.

There are numerous studies with diverse methodologies which may not be possible to summarize in one chapter. We have surveyed some of the studies to give us an insight into the existing studies on household consumption patterns. It has been observed from various studies that consumption patterns have been analyzed by fitting engel curves and estimating expenditure elasticities for various food and non-food items. Linear, double-log, semi-log and log-log-inverse are the common functional forms used for fitting engel curves. Out of these forms, double-logarithmic function has been the most commonly used function to fit engel curve. It is specified as follows:

$$\log y_i = \alpha + b \log x_i$$

Or

$$\log y_i = \alpha + \beta \log x_i + \gamma \log n$$

Where $y_i$ is the expenditure on the ith group of items, $x_i$ is total expenditure (or income), $n$ is family size and $\alpha+\beta$ is used to measure the degrees of economies of scale in consumption. Total consumer expenditure, rather than income, has been usually used as regressor in most of the studies.

It is observed from various studies that some studies emphasized the importance of the methodological issues to analyze household consumption patterns (vide, Leser, 1963; Regmi, *et al.*, 2001; Chern, *et al.*, 2002; Iyengar, 1960; Coondoo, *et al.*, 1969; Bhattacharya and Maitra, 1969); while others analyzed the consumption patterns by fitting one or two accepted forms of engel curve (vide Nisbet & Vakil, 1972; Singh & Singh, 1971; Upender, 1998; Prasad, 2001). The effects of household size on consumption patterns and the existence of economies of scale in consumption have been another area research interest (vide Houthakker, 1957; Gupta, 1968; Iyengar, *et al.*, 1968; Singh, 1973; Nadeem & Khan, 1991). The expenditure elasticities, from all studies, were found to be less than unity for total food items in line with the proposition of engel law and greater than unity for total non-food items.

## 2.2 STUDIES ON CONSUMPTION FUNCTION

### 2.2.1 Brief Review of Global studies

There is a long tradition of theoretical and empirical work on consumption function. Aggregate consumption has featured in macro-models since Keynes in 1936 and is especially important for growth in a transitional economy. Keynes (1936)[40] postulated the consumption function as the relationship between consumption and disposable income. The Keynesian model of consumption takes consumption as a fixed proportion of current income. This is known in consumption literature, as the Absolute Income Hypothesis (AIH). Keynes proposed two hypotheses postulating that the (a) real consumption expenditure is a stable function of real income, and (b) marginal propensity to consume is positive but less than one. Marginal propensity to consume is the ratio of an absolute change in consumption to an absolute change in income.

However, theoretical and empirical limitations of AIH led to the development of the Relative Income Hypothesis (RIH) by Duessenberry (1949), Permanent Income Hypothesis (PIH) by Friedman (1957) and Life-Cycle Hypothesis (LCH) by Brumberg, Modigliani and Ando (1954, 1963).

Duessenberry (1949)[41] argued that current consumption depends not only on the current level of income, but also on the level of consumption attained in previous periods because it is more difficult to reduce a previously attained level of consumption than to reduce saving. More specifically he related average propensity to consume to the ratio of current income to the past peak income.

Friedman (1957)[42] introduces wealth as a major constraint of the consumption function. The permanent income is the income derived from consumer's total wealth. And consumer's current wealth is the present value of the future stream of income from human capital (labor) and other assets. In order to make the theory operational, permanent income must relate to measurable variables. Friedman, therefore, presents a weighted average of current and past values of measured income as a proxy for permanent income. In his permanent income hypothesis, income and consumption are divided into two components each—permanent and transitory. Friedman further assumes that there is no correlation between transitory income and transitory consumption, transitory income and permanent income, and transitory consumption and permanent consumption.

Brumberg and Modigliani, and Modigliani and Ando (1954, 1963)[43], in their life cycle hypothesis, postulated that an individual consumer attempts to maximize utility expressed as a function of lifetime consumption subject to the constraint of the present value of the future stream of income. In order to express the future stream of income in terms of measurable quantities, the expected income stream is divided into expected labour income and income from assets or property. Choosing the right assumptions about expected values and making the right linkage to measurable variables, the consumption function is derived with current labour income and assets as arguments.

Among the three well-known hypotheses after Keynes, permanent income hypothesis of Friedman appears to be one of the best-known relationships and arouses immense research interest in the theory of consumption function. It may be said that the PIH is the best-known relationship that have been postulated between income and consumption (Laumas and Mohabbat, 1972)[44]. Hence, recent literature on the consumption functions has been much dominated by permanent income hypothesis.

Klein and Liviatan (1957)[45] computed regression of the savings-income ratio against several explanatory variables using the 1953 and 1954 Saving Survey data for Great Britain. They chose the proportion of total income received in the form of windfall income (w/y) as one of the explanatory variables. Interestingly, the results of the analysis showed that marginal propensity to consume out of windfall income are significant in all cases that are assumed to be zero in PIH. The marginal propensity to consume out of windfall income was found to be 0.92 for retired persons, 0.65 for employees and 0.74 for upper-income employees. Houthakker (1958)[46], based on the data of family budget survey carried out by the U.S. Bureau of labour Statistics in 1950, also found that marginal propensity to consume out of transitory income is actually greater than marginal propensity to consume out of permanent income. The same evidence has also been found in the works of Bodkin (1950)[47] and Jones (1960)[48].

Kreinin (1961)[49] presented slightly different evidence on expenditure and saving out of windfall gains using data of a 1957-58 survey of Israeli families. He examined the data in various ways including the method used by Bodkin (1959). It was observed in his study that the marginal propensity to consume out of windfall gains to be very low. When durable goods are excluded from consumption, the marginal propensity to consume of non-durables out of windfall income is 0.156. He argued that windfall gain to income might have stimulated the purchase of consumer durables or payment of debts or building up for reserves rather than consumption.

Yang (1964)[50], investigating the consumption behaviour of different countries, made an international comparison of consumption utilizing the data in the Yearbook of National Account Statistics published by United Nations for the Years covering 1957-1960. Eighteen countries, all are market driven economies, were selected for investigation. In this study, he observed that for most of the 18 countries, the level of consumption is highly correlated with the level of current income. When the preceding year's income was introduced as additional variable, an improvement in the goodness of fit in the income-consumption relation was achieved for 8 countries, of which only 4 cases were significant. His investigation also revealed that the degree of instability in the rates of growth in income significantly determines the degree of correlation between income and consumption. The study suggested that the more stable the rate of growth, the higher is the degree of correlation between income and consumption, and vice versa. Further, an examination of the factors determining the consumption-income ratios revealed that only the rate of growth is statistically significant among other factors for which statistical tests were conducted.

Singh and Kumari (1971)[51] examined the applicability of relative income hypothesis in terms of its various specifications proposed by Duessenberry (1949), Duessenberry, Eckstein and Fromm (DEF, 1960) and Davis (1952)[52]. Using the time series data of 10 countries for 1951 through 1968 the analysis was carried out. It was found that relative income hypothesis provides a fairly good representation of the consumption behaviour of all the countries included in the study. All specifications, however, do not perform equally well. The original Deussenberry specification perform very poorly and led them to conclude that the process of habit formation is continuous contrary to what is implied by *Duessenberry's* original specification and that consumption is a better indicator of the standard of living than income.

Hall (1978)[53] took the Life cycle-permanent income approach and applied Rational Expectations Hypothesis (REH). Specifically, the REH implies that people behave as though they have knowledge of the process of generating income. On the basis of this reasoning, the theory assumes that people will not change their level of consumption unless new information causes them to revise their future expectation of income. He argued that the underlying behaviour of consumers makes both consumption and wealth evolve as a random walk since marginal utility evolves as a random walk with trend. According to Hall, for permanent income hypothesis or life cycle hypothesis (under REH) to be consistent with data, all coefficients for lagged variables except for that of the first lag consumption must be statistically insignificant. Using quarterly US data, Hall shows that lags of consumption beyond the first lag were not significant. However, his results also show marginal evidence that recent lags of disposable income had predictive powers for consumption, and stronger evidence in favour of lagged measures of wealth such as price of shares.

Davidson, Hendry, Srba and Yeo (1978)[54] made another influential approach called DHSY error correction model of consumption. They present a dynamic time series model of consumption based on the underlying long run equilibrium relationship between consumption and income. In this approach, it is assumed that the long run relationship during any point in time between income and consumption may be out of equilibrium. This suggests that consumers take time to adjust to changes in income. On the contrary, if such time allowances did not take place, the adjustment would take place instantaneously.

Davis (1984)[55], having to test a number of alternative consumption models, proved the empirical evidence of the DHSY model and concluded that the DHSY model is the best specification for United Kingdom.

Molana (1990)[56] also applied the error correction model (ECM) approach and concluded that the ECM would be appropriate in specifying the relationship between consumption and wealth. In another study, Chambers (1991)[57] applies the same approach and finds the ECM to produce good forecasts for the UK economy.

Flavin (1981)[58] revisits *Hall's* hypothesis using a structural econometric model of consumption based on the innovation process in income driving changes in consumption. She finds that consumption is more sensitive to changes in income than proposed by the permanent income hypothesis or life cycle hypothesis.

Campbell and Mankiw (1990)[59] also find little support for permanent income hypothesis. They, further, found that about 50 per cent of the consumers in United States based their consumption decisions on current income and this findings appears to offer an alternative theory to and wrench out of context in the permanent income hypothesis.

Besides the determinants of consumption discussed so far, it was also found in several studies, Muellbauer and Lattimore (1995)[60], Zeldes (1989)[61] and Blinder and Deaton (1985)[62] that in the advanced industrialized countries consumption are also determined by additional variables such as demographic factors, liquidity constraints and uncertainty.

Sameroynina (2005)[63] attempted to study the consumption and saving behaviour in Russia using the data of Russian Longitudinal Monitoring Survey for the years between 1994 and 2002. He found that: (1) the saving rate had been steadily decreasing since 1994 and significantly dropped in 1998. However, the saving rate as measured by the standard definition has increased a little in 2002, (2) no significant correlation between changes in consumption and past changes in income. However, changes in consumption are significantly related to lag changes in savings and expenditures on durables; and (3) changes in income are negatively correlated with lagged changes in saving. Therefore, saving is an important predictor of future income alterations as the permanent income hypothesis predicts.

### 2.2.2 Brief Review of Studies in India

Narasimham (1956)[64], using linear regression, estimated the marginal propensity to consume in India for different categories of income. His estimates were: 0.96 for farm income and 0.86 for non-corporate business income. Iyengar and Moorthy (1959)[65] also made three estimates for the marginal propensity to consume, from the models that they fitted to time series data relating to national accounts, namely, 0.606, 0.718 and 0.717.

Roy Choudhury (1968)[66] made a thorough examination of consumption and saving functions for India utilizing the data of the Reserve Bank of India's Series of Savings and Consumption and the data of National Sample Survey Organization. She tried out several alternative functional forms with and without lagged explanatory variables, and some of the important findings are as follows: (1) aggregate income seems to be a better explanatory variable than per capita income, and among the functional forms a simple straight line with no other explanatory variables seems to give the best result; (2) the propensities seem to differ widely between urban and rural areas; (3) from the results of fits to lagged variables, it was observed that factors other than current year's income have hardly any influence in determining the current level of consumption; and (4) the fits are generally less good for the urban sector than for the rural sector.

Gupta (1970)[67], criticizing the work of Roy Choudhury (1968), made certain alternative exercises and arrived at much more acceptable results. It was found in his study that: (1) there is significant effect of price changes and wealth on total and urban per capita consumption; (2) contrary to the findings of *Roy Choudhury's* negative propensity to consume out of permanent income for the urban sector, it was observed that there is positive marginal propensity to consume equal to about 0.62; and (3) there is much stronger support for the permanent income hypothesis.

Mammon (1982)[68] attempted to estimate the consumption function for India for a much longer period using the data of National Account Statistics for the period of 1950-51 to 1978-79. His study presents an evidence of lagged response of consumption to disposable income in case of India. Further, it lends some support to a general consensus view that the household's net saving rate is around 15 per cent of disposable income.

Upender (1996)[69], using the data of various issues of Economic Survey and National Accounts Statistics covering the period of 1950-51 to 1990-91, made an exercise to estimate the short-run and long-run consumption function for India. It can be observed from his exercise that the autonomous consumption expenditure is greater than zero showing the presence of dis-savings of Indian households at lower income levels. The marginal propensity to consume was positive and less than unity evincing that the consumption expenditure was increasing with an increase in income but not by as much as income. The MPC was less than the average propensity to consume showing that the short-run elasticity of consumption expenditure was less than unity. The long-run elasticity of consumption expenditure was found to be substantially greater than the short-run elasticity of consumption expenditure corroborating the economic assumption that the long-run MPC is bound to be higher than the short-run MPC due to discrepancy between actual change and desired change in consumption expenditure.

Prasad (2001)[70] calculated the value of average propensity to consume and marginal propensity to consume in India using the data of National Account Statistics published by Central Statistical Organization, Government of India for the period of 1950-51 to 1996-97. He divided the whole period under study into seven periods. He observed that the calculated APC and MPC did not strictly confirm the properties of the Absolute Income Hypothesis as proposed by Keynes (1936). As saving is the residual of the personal income, the declining APC implies that the increase in Average Propensity to Save. This implies that with increasing personal disposable income, less proportion will be devoted to consumption and a greater proportion to savings as income increases. Accordingly, he suggested that the government had to provide more tax exemptions so that the income at the disposal of the households and in returns the saving will increase. He observed that the APC had declined from 0.94 in 1950-51 to 0.75 in 1996-97. The Marginal Propensity to Consume calculated using Linear and Double-Log function did not show any clear pattern for the study period. The MPC varies between 2.16 and 0.47 during the whole study period. He observed that both MPC and APC tend to fall and to rise together but the changes in APC are more regular than the changes occurred in MPC. And the fall in MPC is steeper than the fall in APC.

Studies of consumption function are generally the extension and testing of the three well-known hypotheses namely Absolute Income Hypothesis by Keynes (1936), Relative Income Hypothesis by Duessenbery (1949) and Permanent Income Hypothesis by Friedman (1957). Out of these, the Permanent Income Hypothesis appears to be the best-known relationship which arose immense research though the assumption of zero marginal propensities to consume out of windfall income under PIH was disapproved in some studies including the Klein and Liviatan (1957), Houthakker (1958), Bodkin (1959), Jones (1960). The marginal propensity to consume, in all studies, is usually estimated by linear and double-log regression, though some of the studies, Singh and Kumari (1971)—DEF model, Hall (1978)—REH model and Davidson, *et al.* (1978)—DHSY model, used slightly complicated models.

## NOTES

1. Ducpetiaux, Edouard (1855): *Budget economiques des classes ouvrieres en Belgique.* Brussel.
2. *Ibid.*
3. Engel, Ernst (1857): *Die Production and Consumtionswerhalt nisse des Konigreichs Sachsen.* Dresden.
4. Schwabe, Hermann (1868): Das Verhaltniss Von Miethe und Einkommen in Berlin. *Statistical Yearbook of Berlin*, pp. 264-67.
5. Wright, Caroll (1875): *Sixth Annual Report of the Bureau of labour Statistics.* Boston, pp. 441.
6. Vecchio, Del (1912): *Relazioni fra entrata e consume.* Giornale degli economisti, ser XLIV, pp. 111-42
7. Stigler, George J. (1954): The Early History of Empirical Studies of Consumer Behaviour. *The Journal of Political Economy*, Vol. LXII, April, pp. 95-113.
8. Leser, C.E.V. (1941): Family Budget Data and Price-Elasticities of Demand. *The Review of Economic Studies*, Vol. 9, No. 1, November, pp. 40-57.
9. Burk, Marguerite C. (1951): Changes in the Demand for Food from 1941 to 1950. *Journal of Farm Economics*. Vol. 33, No. 3 (Aug.), pp. 281-29.
10. Houthakker, H.S. (1957): An International Comparison of Household Expenditure Patterns, Commemorating the Centenary of Engel's Law. *Econometrica*, Vol. 25, No. 4 (Oct.), pp. 532-551.
11. Leser, C.E.V. (1963): Forms of Engel Functions. *Econometrica*, Vol. 31, No. 4 (October), pp. 694-703.
12. Nisbet, Charles T. and Firouz Vakil (1972): Some Estimates of Prices and Expenditure Elasticities of Demand for Marijuana Among UCLA Students. *The Review of Economics and Statistics*, Vol. 54, No. 4 (Nov.), pp. 473-475.
13. Nadeem A. Burney, Ashfaque H. Khan (1991): Household consumption patterns in Pakistan: an urban-rural comparison using micro data. *Pakistan Development Review*, Summer.
14. Economic Research Service (1997): *Changing Structure of Global Food Consumption and Trade.* Working Paper No. 01-1.
15. Regmi, Anita; M.S. Deepak; James L. Seale Jr. and Jason Bernstein (2001): *Cross-Country Analysis of Food Consumption Patterns.* Diane Publishing Co., Darby.

16. Theil, Henry; Ching-Fan, Chung and James L. Scale Jr (1989): *International Evidence on Consumption Patterns.* Greenwich, CT: JAI Press Inc.
17. Lanfranco, Bruno A.; Ames, Glenn W.C. and Huang, Chung L. (2000): *Food Demand Elasticities of the US Hispanic Community.* Paper presented at IAAE XXIV Conference, Berlin, August 13-18.
18. Chern, Wen S., Kimiko Ishibashi, Kiyoshi Taniguchi and Yuki Tokoyama (2002): *Analysis of Food Consumption Behaviour By Japanese Households.* Agriculture and Development Economic Division of the Food and Agriculture Organization, Working Paper No. 206. www.fao.org/es/esa
19. The Provincial Decision-Making Enabling (PROVIDE) Project on *Household expenditure patterns in South Africa-1995 (Background Paper 2003: 2)*, Elsenburg September 2003
20. Burger, Ronelle (2004); van der Berg, Servaas and Nieftagodien, Sihaam: *Consumption Patterns of South Africa.s Rising Black Middle-Class: Correcting for Measurement Errors.* Paper presented at the conference of the 'Centre for the Study of African Economies (CSAE) on Poverty Reduction, Growth and Human Development in Africa'. Oxford, March.
21. Kushwaha, S. Sen, Chandra and Yakasai M.T. (2007): Current Trends in Vegetalbe Consumption in Nigeria: A case study of consumption pattern in Kano State. Paper presented at the I Mediterranean Conference of Agro-Food Social Scientists. 103rd EAAE Seminar '*Adding Value to the Agro-Food Supply Chain in the Future Euromediterranean Space*'. Barcelona, Spain, April 23rd-25th.
22. Roy, J. and Laha, R.G. (1960): *Preliminary Estimates of relative increase in consumer demand in rural and urban India.* In 'Studies on Consumer Behaviour'. Asia publishing House, Bombay.
23. Iyengar, Sreenivasa N. (1960): On a Method of Computing Engel Elasticities from Concentration Curves. *Econometrica*, Vol. 28, No. 4, (Oct.), pp. 882-891.
24. Sinha, R.P. (1966): An Analysis of Food Expenditure in India. *Journal of Farm Economics*, Vol. 48, No. 1 (Feb.), pp. 113-123.
25. Iyengar, N.S., L.R. Jain and T.N. Srinivasan (1968).: Economies of Scale in Household Consumption: A Case Study. *Indian Economic Journal*, 15, *Econometric Annual*, pp. 465-477.

26. Gupta, D.B. (1968): A Comparison of Consumption Patterns *in Uttar Pradesh and Madras—A study of inter-regional variations with reference to India. Indian Economic Review*, New Series, 3, pp. 129-144.
27. Maitra, T. (1969): *On Regional and Temporal Variation in Engel Curves in rural India.* ISI Technical Report No. Econ/2/69.
28. Bhattacharya, N. and Maitra, T. (1969): *An Analysis of engel curves based on NSS household budget data for the 7th to 22nd rounds.* A paper presented to the 10th Indian Econometric Conference, Madurai.
29. Singh, Balbir (1973): *The effects of household composition on its consumption. A case study.* Sankhya, Series B, 35.
30. Coondoo, Dipankor (1969): *The Effect of Relative Prices on Engel Elasticity of Cereals in India.* Arthaniti, Vol. 12.
31. Singh, Amarjit and Haramol Singh (1971): Changing Consumption Pattern in Punjab: Projections of Consumer Demand for 1973-74. *Economic and Political Weekly*, Vol. VI, No. 50.
32. Jain, L.R. and Tendulkar, S.D. (1972): *An Empirical Evaluation of the System of addilog engel curves.* Paper Presented at the 12th Indian Econometrics Conference, Kanpur.
33. Coondoo, Dipankor (1975): A comparison of consumer expenditure pattern of Indian middle class and working class families. Sankhya: *The Indian Journal of Statistics*. Vol. 37, Series C, Pt. 2, pp. 81-101.
34. Coondoo, Dipankor; Robin Mukherjee and D.S. Prasada Rao (1981): Engel Curve Analysis with Non-Monetized Consumption. *The Journal of Income and Wealth*, Vol. 5, No. 2, July.
35. Upender, M. (1998): Estimates of Expenditure Elasticities of Demand. *Finance India*, Vol. XII, No. 3, September.
36. Upender, M. (1999): Expenditure Elasticity for Clothing. *Anvesak*, Vol. 29, No. 2, December.
37. Prasad, A.R. (2001): *Consumption Behaviour in India: Theory and Evidence.* Reliance Publishing House, New Delhi, pp. 342-343.
38. Gangopadhyay, Shubhashis and Wadhwa, Wilima (2004): *Changing Pattern of Household Consumption Expenditure. (SERFA)* August.
39. Ghose, Suchismita and Nikhilesh Bhattacharya (1995): Effect

of Reference Period on Engel Elasticities of Clothing and Other Items: Further Results. Sankhya: *The Indian Journal of Statistics*, Vol. 57, Series B, Pt. 3, pp. 433-449.

40. Keynes, J.M. (1936): *The General Theory of Employment, Interest and Money*. Macmillan, New York.
41. Duessenberry, James (1949): *Income, Saving and the Theory of Consumer Behaviour*. Harvard University Press, Cambridge, Massachussets, 1967.
42. Friedman, Milton (1957): *A Theory of Consumption Function*. Oxford and IBH Publishing Co. New Delhi, 1970.
43. Modigliani, Franco and Richard Brumberg (1963): *Utility Analysis and Consumption Function: An Interpretation of Cross section data.* Post Keynesian Economics, Rutgers Univ. Press. Pp. 388-436; and Modigliani, F. and A. Ando: The Life Cycle Hypothesis of Saving: Aggregate Implications and Tests. *American Economic Review*, Vol. 53, (1963) pp. 56-83.
44. Laumas, Prem S. and Khan A. Mohabbat (1972): The Permanent Income Hypothesis: Evidence from Time Series Data. *The American Economic Review*, Vol. 62, No. 4 (Sept.) pp. 730.
45. Kreinin, M.E. (1961): Windfall Income and Consumption—Additional Evidence. *American Economic Review*, Vol. 51 (June), pp. 388-90.
46. Houthakker, H.S. (1958): The Permanent Income Hypothesis. *American Economic Review*, June, pp398.
47. Bodkin, R.G. (1959): Windfall Income and Consumption. *American Economic Review*, September, pp. 602-14.
48. Bodkin, Ronald (1959): Windfall Income and Consumption. *American Economic Review*. Vol. 49 (Sept.,) pp. 602-14.
49. Kreinin, M.E. (1961): Windfall Income and Consumption—Additional Evidence. *American Economic Review*, Vol. 51 (June), pp. 388-90.
50. Yang, Charles Yneu (1964): An International Comparison of Consumption Functions. *The Review of Economics and Statistics*, Vol. 46, No. 3 (Aug.) pp. 279-286.
51. Singh, Balbir and Ramesh C. Kumari (1971): The Relative Income Hypothesis—A Cross Country Analysis. *The Review of Income and Wealth*, Series 17. pp. 341-348.
52. Davis, T.E. (1952): The Consumption Function as Tool for Prediction. *Review of Economic Statistics*, Vol. 34, pp. 270-77.
53. Hall, R.E. (1978): Stochastic Implications of the Life Cycle

Hypothesis: Theory and Evidence. *Journal of Political Economy*, Vol. 86, pp. 971-987.

54. Davidson, J.E.H., D.F. Hendry., F. Srba and S. Yeo (1978): Econometric Modelling of Aggregate Time Series Relationship between Consumers, Expenditure and Income in United Kingdom. *The Economic Journal*, Vol. 88, pp. 661-692.
55. Davis, M.A. (1984): The Consumption Function in Macroeconomic Models: A comparative study. *Applied Economics*, Vol. 16., pp. 799-838.
56. Molana, H. (1990): The Time Series Consumption Function: Error Correction, Random Walk and Steady State. *The Economic Journal*, Vol. 101, pp. 383-402.
57. Chambers, M.J. (1991): An Alternative Time Series Model of Consumption: Some empirical Evidence. *Applied Economics*, Vol. 23, pp. 1361-66.
58. Flavin, M. (1981): The Adjustment of Consumption to Changing Expectations about future income. *Journal of Political Economy*, Vol. 89, No. 5, pp. 974-1009.
59. Campbell, J. and N. Mankiw (1990): Permanent Income, Current Income and Consumption. *Journal of Business and Economic Statistics*, Vol. 8, pp. 265-279.
60. Muellbauer, J. and R. Lattimore (1995): The Consumption Function: A Theoretical and Empirical Overview. *Handbook of Applied Econometrics*, Vol. 1: Macroeconomics edited by M.H. Wickens, Oxford.
61. Zeldes, S.P. (1989): Consumption and Liquidity Constraints: An Empirical Investigation. *Journal of Political Economy*, Vol. 97, pp. 305-345.
62. Blinder, A.R. and A. Deaton (1985): *Time Series Consumption Function Revisited.* Brookings paper on Economic Activity, Vol. 2, pp. 465-521.
63. Sameroyanina, Yuliana (2005): *Consumption and Saving Behaviour in Russia.* Working Paper, Columbia University, March.
64. Narasimham, N.V.A. (1956): *A Short-Term Planning Model for India.* North Holland Publishing Co., Amsterdam.
65. Iyengar, N.S. and S. Krishna Moorty (1959): On Some Econometric Models of India. *Arthaniti*, Vol. 2.
66. Roy Choudhury, Uma Datta (1968): Income, Consumption and Saving in Urban and Rural India. *The Review of Income and Wealth, Series* 14, No. 1 (March) pp. 37-56.

67. Gupta, K.L. (1970): Income, Consumption and Saving in Urban and Rural India: *A Note. The Review of Income and Wealth*, Series 16, No. 4 (Dec.) pp. 377-388.
68. Mammon, Thampy (1982): Consumption Function: Some Further Tests. *The Indian Economic Journal*, Vol. 30, No. 1 (July-Sept.) pp. 15-22.
69. Upender, M. (1996): The Short and Long Run Aggregate Consumption Functions. *Indian Journal of Applied Economics*, Vol. 5, No. 2, Jan-March.
70. Prasad, A.R. (2001): *Consumption Behaviour in India: Theory and Evidence*. Reliance Publishing House, New Delhi.

# 3
# General Pattern of Consumer Expenditure in North-Eastern India

Private final consumption expenditure in a readily quantifiable form is a direct measure of the standard of living of thc people. As a criterion for evaluating the index of human well being, it is much more meaningful than domestic product or per capita income when the purpose is to understand the effect of domestic product on the condition of living of the population (Prasad, 2001)[1]. With the development of the economy, the pattern of consumer expenditure changes in which the share of food items decreases. At the same time, the share of non-food items—including consumption goods and services—increases with the increase in the level of income. The changing share of food items is described by Engel's Law which states 'the poorer a family, the greater the proportion of its total expenditure that must be devoted to the provision of food' (Stigler, 1954)[2].

Since food is vital to life, the ratio of food consumption to total income or expenditure provides a basis for comparing the economic conditions of the country with that of other countries. Several studies (Theil, *et al.*, 1989; Cranfield, *et al.*, 1998 and Regmi, *et al.*, 2001)[3] confirmed that low-income countries spend a greater proportion (50% or more) of their total expenditure on food compared with richer countries, which spend less than 20 per cent of their total expenditure on food. In general, it has been observed that lower income countries spend a greater proportion of their budget on necessities such as food, while richer countries spend a greater proportion on luxuries.

In line with the plan of our study, this chapter deals with the patterns of consumer expenditure in North-Eastern India/Region (NER) and Mizoram. Consumer expenditure data for the states of NER are obtained from the Reports of various rounds of NSS, Ministry of Statistics and Programme Implementation, Government of India. At the same time, the general pattern of consumer expenditure in Mizoram has been analyzed from the data of our sample survey.

## 3.1 TREND OF MONTHLY PER CAPITA CONSUMER EXPENDITURE (MPCE) IN NORTH-EASTERN REGION

An analysis of the trend of MPCE at constant price for a long period of time would enable us to know the impact of economic development on the improvement of the standard of living of the people in the country. The trends of MPCE in NER for 10 years (i.e. 1994-95 to 2005-06) at current prices and constant price have been given in Table 3.1 and Table 3.2 respectively.

The MPCE at current prices in rural areas of NER have continuously increased from Rs. 378.74 in 1994-95 to Rs. 1081 in 2005-06. Similarly, urban MPCE have also increased from Rs. 492.28 in 1994-95 to Rs. 1875 in 2005-06. The absolute difference of rural and urban per capita consumption in NER has been increasing during the period under study. In other words, rural-urban differences have been continuously increasing. The ratio of rural MPCE to urban MPCE or rural MPCE as a percentage of urban MPCE have shown a decreasing trend with the compound rate of annual decay of –2.20 per cent.

**Table 3.1:** Trend of Average Rural and Urban Monthly Per Capita Expenditure (MPCE) in North-Eastern India and India at Current Prices (in Rs)

| *Year* | *NSS Round* | *North-Eastern India* | | | *India* | | |
|---|---|---|---|---|---|---|---|
| | | *Rural* | *Urban* | *Rural as % of Urban* | *Rural* | *Urban* | *Rural as % of Urban* |
| 1994-95 | 51 | 378.74 | 492.28 | 76.94 | 309.43 | 508.07 | 60.90 |
| 1995-96 | 52 | 411.64 | 605.46 | 67.99 | 344.29 | 599.26 | 57.45 |
| 1998 | 54 | 477.35 | 697.64 | 68.42 | 382.07 | 684.27 | 55.84 |
| 1999-00 | 55 | 612.34 | 917.62 | 66.73 | 486.07 | 854.96 | 56.85 |
| 2000-01 | 56 | 619.86 | 988.35 | 62.72 | 494.90 | 914.57 | 54.11 |
| 2001-02 | 57 | 603.47 | 987.79 | 61.09 | 498.27 | 932.79 | 53.42 |
| 2002 | 58 | 627.73 | 1068.95 | 58.72 | 544.57 | 1011.97 | 53.81 |
| 2003 | 59 | 662.65 | 1008.44 | 65.71 | 554.15 | 1021.89 | 54.23 |
| 2004 | 60 | 718.33 | 1128.35 | 63.66 | 616.57 | 1149.52 | 53.64 |
| 2005-06 | 62 | 1081.00 | 1875.00 | 57.65 | 624.53 | 1170.00 | 53.38 |
| CAGR (%) | | 10.06 | 12.00 | (–)2.20 | 7.94 | 9.25 | (–)1.2 |

**Table 3.2:** Trend of Average Rural and Urban Monthly Per Capita Expenditure (MPCE) in North-Eastern India and India at Constant Price (1993-94=100) (in Rs)

| *Year* | *NSS Round* | *North-Eastern India* | | | *India* | | |
|---|---|---|---|---|---|---|---|
| | | *Rural* | *Urban* | *Rural as % of Urban* | *Rural* | *Urban* | *Rural as % of Urban* |
| 1994-95 | 51 | 329.72 | 426.30 | 77.34 | 268.82 | 438.84 | 61.26 |
| 1995-96 | 52 | 324.36 | 472.31 | 68.68 | 270.84 | 466.52 | 58.06 |
| 1998 | 54 | 310.62 | 455.96 | 68.13 | 248.75 | 447.86 | 55.54 |
| 1999-00 | 55 | 393.06 | 596.38 | 65.91 | 312.46 | 558.81 | 55.91 |
| 2000-01 | 56 | 387.84 | 627.86 | 61.77 | 311.06 | 585.80 | 53.10 |
| 2001-02 | 57 | 364.81 | 606.63 | 60.14 | 302.07 | 575.40 | 52.50 |
| 2002 | 58 | 370.91 | 638.91 | 58.05 | 323.52 | 607.72 | 53.24 |
| 2003 | 59 | 364.84 | 554.88 | 65.75 | 305.08 | 562.07 | 54.28 |
| 2004 | 60 | 383.68 | 601.34 | 63.80 | 328.99 | 611.18 | 53.83 |
| 2005-06 | 62 | 583.43 | 1012.96 | 57.60 | 333.27 | 631.93 | 52.74 |
| CAGR (%) | | 4.26 | 6.68 | (–)2.28 | 2.70 | 4.04 | (–)1.29 |

It has also been observed that the national average of rural MPCE (at current prices) increased from Rs. 309.43 in 1994-95 to Rs. 624.53 in 2005-06. Urban MPCE also increased from Rs. 508.90 to Rs. 1170.00 during the same period. The same trend has been observed in case of rural-urban differences in per capita consumption in India as it is in NER. Rural MPCE as a per cent of urban MPCE has decreased from 60.90 per cent in 1994-95 to 53.38 per cent in 2005-06. The rate of changes in the ratio of rural-urban difference is lower in India (i.e. –1.2%) than in NER (i.e. –2.20%).

We have observed that the average MPCE have been increasing in all areas under study. However, the increase in per capita consumption may be due price increase or inflation. To remove the effect of price rise, we deflate each of the MPCE by the corresponding Wholesale Price Index (1993-94 as base year), for food and nonfood items to obtain MPCE at constant price. Further, the changes in per capita consumption at constant price would reflect the improvement or increase in the standard of living or real consumption of the people.

The average per capita consumption at constant price in rural areas of NER has increased from Rs. 329.72 in 1994-95 to Rs. 583.43 in 2005-06 while urban per capita consumption increased from Rs. 426.30 to

Rs. 1017.99 during the same period. The compound annual growth rate of rural MPCE and urban MPCE at constant price are 4.26 per cent and 6.68 per cent respectively. In other words, the overall increased in real consumption in NER are 76.9 per cent and 138.8 per cent for rural areas and urban areas respectively. The average of rural per capita consumption at constant price in India has increased from Rs. 268.82 in 1994-95 to Rs. 333.27 with compound annual growth rate of 2.70 per cent; while urban average has increased from Rs. 438.84 to Rs. 631.93 with compound annual growth rate of 4.04 per cent.

A notable feature of the analysis of the trend of MPCE in NER and India is the continuously increasing gap between rural and urban per capita consumption. The difference may be due to the price differentials between the two areas. Price differences between rural and urban areas are quite evident in the study made by Bhattacharya and Chatterjee (1971)[4] and Bhattacharya and Joshi (1980)[5]. However, even after taking into account the price differentials to the tune of 25 per cent[6] (i.e. urban is 25% higher than rural MPCE), rural-urban differences are still considerable for NER as well as India as a whole.

## 3.2 CHANGING PATTERN OF CONSUMER EXPENDITURE IN NORTH-EASTERN REGION

It is a well known fact that the share of food items in the total consumer expenditure declines as the total income or expenditure increases. In other words, the share of food items declines with the improvement of the standard of living of the people. Indian economy has undergone a significant improvement of standard of living especially after the Economic Reform in 1991. In order to understand the effect of economic development on the standard of living of North Eastern Region after 1991, the trend of the per capita consumer expenditure on food and nonfood items—including 'cereals and cereals substitutes' within food items and 'pan, tobacco and intoxicants', 'fuel and light', 'clothing and footwear' and 'education' within nonfood items—have been analyzed in this section. The whole series of data are obtained from the Reports of various rounds of NSS.

The rural per capita expenditure on food at current prices, presented in Table 3.3, has increased from Rs. 241.65 in 1994-95 to Rs. 436.10 in 2005-06 with compound annual growth rate of 6.41 per cent; while nonfood items increased from Rs. 137.08 to Rs. 645.00 with the compound annual growth rate (CAGR) of 14.41 per cent. The rate of growth of expenditure on nonfood items is more than two times the growth rate of food items reflecting the structural changes of per capita consumer expenditure in NER from food to nonfood items with the process of economic development. Within food items the item group of 'cereals and cereals substitutes' has increased, with CAGR of 2.6 per cent, from Rs. 108.72 to Rs. 151.00 during the study period. Among nonfood items, the rate of growth of per capita expenditure has been found to be the lowest in education (i.e. CAGR of 1.48%) followed by 'pan, tobacco and intoxicants' (4.65%); while the growth of per capita expenditure on 'clothing and footwear' (14.14%) is the highest followed by 'fuel and light' (9.27%). Lower rate of growth in case of education may be attributable to the governmental efforts to deliver free education for all children through various projects like Sarva Siksha Abyan.

In urban areas, per capita expenditure on food increased from Rs. 279.80 in 1994-95 to Rs. 620.70 in 2005-06 with CAGR of 8.25; while nonfood expenditure has increased from Rs. 212.47 to Rs. 1254 with CAGR of 12.71 per cent. The rate of increased of 'cereals and cereals substitutes' is 8.5 per cent against the rural growth rate of 2.6 per cent. Within nonfood group, the highest rate of growth of expenditure in urban areas is found in case of education (16.32) followed by 'pan,

**Table 3.3:** Average Monthly Expenditure (in Rs) Per Person in Rural Areas of North-Eastern India (At Current Prices)

| *Year* | *NSS Round* | *Cereals and Cereals Substitutes* | *Food Total* | *Pan, Tobacco and Intoxicants* | *Fuel and Light* | *Clothing and Footwear* | *Education* | *Nonfood Total* | *Total Consumer Expenditure* |
|---|---|---|---|---|---|---|---|---|---|
| 1994-95 | 51 | 108.72 | 241.65 | 33.83 | 39.67 | 13.55 | 9.47 | 137.08 | 378.74 |
| 1995-96 | 52 | 116.32 | 254.95 | 20.30 | 31.00 | 38.38 | 18.90 | 156.70 | 411.64 |
| 1998 | 54 | 133.32 | 295.26 | 22.24 | 37.60 | 27.91 | 34.99 | 182.08 | 477.35 |
| 1999-00 | 55 | 155.53 | 369.76 | 32.53 | 52.53 | 46.94 | 18.70 | 242.58 | 612.34 |
| 2000-01 | 56 | 159.73 | 367.13 | 28.53 | 55.15 | 50.98 | 24.53 | 252.73 | 619.86 |
| 2001-02 | 57 | 148.56 | 346.69 | 25.29 | 48.21 | 52.52 | 27.20 | 256.78 | 603.47 |
| 2002 | 58 | 140.22 | 352.44 | 31.19 | 58.31 | 59.97 | 25.55 | 275.29 | 627.73 |
| 2003 | 59 | 140.54 | 365.19 | 30.67 | 60.61 | 61.20 | 4.46 | 297.45 | 662.65 |
| 2004 | 60 | 135.04 | 441.09 | 42.86 | 57.18 | 48.87 | 24.63 | 277.24 | 718.33 |
| 2005-06 | 62 | 151 | 436.1 | 38.24 | 85.75 | 64.81 | 29.27 | 645.00 | 1081.10 |
| CGR (%) | | 2.6 | 6.41 | 4.67 | 9.27 | 14.14 | 1.48 | 14.41 | 10.06 |

**Table 3.4:** Average Monthly Expenditure (in Rs) Per Person in Urban Areas of North-Eastern India (At Current Prices)

| *Year* | *NSS Round* | *Cereals and Cereals Substitutes* | *Food Total* | *Pan, Tobacco and Intoxicants* | *Fuel and Light* | *Clothing and Footwear* | *Education* | *Nonfood Total* | *Total Consumer Expenditure* |
|---|---|---|---|---|---|---|---|---|---|
| 1994-95 | 51 | 109.65 | **279.8** | 22.72 | 38.12 | 43.16 | 25.94 | **212.47** | 492.28 |
| 1995-96 | 52 | 115.49 | **315.21** | 28.8 | 41.65 | 53.8 | 44.28 | **290.25** | 605.46 |
| 1998 | 54 | 135.46 | **367.31** | 26.15 | 46.97 | 33.92 | 71.74 | **330.33** | 697.64 |
| 1999-00 | 55 | 158.2 | **476.65** | 40.53 | 60.53 | 69.3 | 44.16 | **440.97** | 917.62 |
| 2000-01 | 56 | 172.92 | **486.84** | 35.64 | 78.92 | 83.88 | 60.62 | **501.51** | 988.35 |
| 2001-02 | 57 | 152.18 | **457.48** | 35.46 | 77.21 | 89.31 | 62.41 | **530.32** | 987.79 |
| 2002 | 58 | 153.27 | **497.01** | 43.39 | 89.2 | 101.34 | 62.11 | **571.95** | 1068.95 |
| 2003 | 59 | 149.91 | **472.57** | 33.41 | 85.78 | 90.32 | 6.9 | **535.88** | 1008.44 |
| 2004 | 60 | 154.38 | **608.2** | 45.57 | 82.18 | 74.39 | 62.05 | **520.15** | 1128.35 |
| 2005-06 | 62 | 156.8 | **620.7** | 55.13 | 123.6 | 103.8 | 75.88 | **1254** | 1875.70 |
| CGR (%) | 3.6 | 8.5 | 8.25 | 13.31 | 11.15 | 4.58 | 16.32 | 12.71 | 12.00 |

**Table 3.5:** Percentage Distribution of Total Consumer Expenditure Per Person Per Month Over Groups of Items of Consumption for Rural Areas of North-Eastern India (Current Prices)

| *Year* | *NSS Round* | *Cereals and Cereals Substitutes* | *Food Total* | *Pan, Tobacco and Intoxicants* | *Fuel and Light* | *Clothing and Footwear* | *Education* | *Nonfood Total* | *Total Consumer Expenditure* |
|---|---|---|---|---|---|---|---|---|---|
| 1994-95 | 51 | 28.71 | **63.80** | 8.93 | 10.47 | 3.58 | 2.50 | 36.19 | 100.00 |
| 1995-96 | 52 | 28.26 | **61.94** | 4.93 | 7.53 | 9.32 | 4.59 | 38.07 | 100.00 |
| 1998 | 54 | 27.93 | **61.85** | 4.66 | 7.88 | 5.85 | 7.33 | 38.14 | 100.00 |
| 1999-00 | 55 | 25.40 | **60.38** | 5.31 | 8.58 | 7.67 | 3.05 | 39.62 | 100.00 |
| 2000-01 | 56 | 25.77 | **59.23** | 4.60 | 8.90 | 8.22 | 3.96 | 40.77 | 100.00 |
| 2001-02 | 57 | 24.62 | **57.45** | 4.19 | 7.99 | 8.70 | 4.51 | 42.55 | 100.00 |
| 2002 | 58 | 22.34 | **56.15** | 4.97 | 9.29 | 9.55 | 4.07 | 43.85 | 100.00 |
| 2003 | 59 | 21.21 | **55.11** | 4.63 | 9.15 | 9.24 | 0.67 | 44.89 | 100.00 |
| 2004 | 60 | 18.80 | **61.40** | 5.97 | 7.96 | 6.80 | 3.43 | 38.60 | 100.00 |
| 2005-06 | 62 | 13.97 | **40.34** | 3.54 | 7.93 | 5.99 | 2.71 | 59.66 | 100.00 |

**Table 3.6:** Percentage Distribution of Total Consumer Expenditure Per Person Per Month Over Groups of Items of Consumption for Urban are Groups of Items of Consumption for Urban Areas of North-Eastern India (Current Prices)

| *Year* | *NSS Round* | *Cereals and Cereals Substitutes* | *Food Total* | *Pan, Tobacco and Intoxicants* | *Fuel and Light* | *Clothing and Footwear* | *Education* | *Nonfood Total* | *Total Consumer Expenditure* |
|---|---|---|---|---|---|---|---|---|---|
| 1994-95 | 51 | 22.27 | **56.84** | 4.62 | 7.74 | 8.77 | 5.27 | 43.16 | 100.00 |
| 1995-96 | 52 | 19.07 | **52.06** | 4.76 | 6.88 | 8.89 | 7.31 | 47.94 | 100.00 |
| 1998 | 54 | 19.42 | **52.65** | 3.75 | 6.73 | 4.86 | 10.28 | 47.35 | 100.00 |
| 1999-00 | 55 | 17.24 | **51.94** | 4.42 | 6.60 | 7.55 | 4.81 | 48.06 | 100.00 |
| 2000-01 | 56 | 17.50 | **49.26** | 3.61 | 7.99 | 8.49 | 6.13 | 50.74 | 100.00 |
| 2001-02 | 57 | 15.41 | **46.31** | 3.59 | 7.82 | 9.04 | 6.32 | 53.69 | 100.00 |
| 2002 | 58 | 14.34 | **46.50** | 4.06 | 8.34 | 9.48 | 5.81 | 53.51 | 100.00 |
| 2003 | 59 | 14.87 | **46.86** | 3.31 | 8.51 | 8.96 | 0.68 | 53.14 | 100.00 |
| 2004 | 60 | 13.68 | **53.90** | 4.04 | 7.28 | 6.59 | 5.50 | 46.10 | 100.00 |
| 2005-06 | 62 | 8.36 | **33.09** | 2.94 | 6.59 | 5.53 | 4.05 | 66.86 | 100.00 |

tobacco and intoxicants' (13.31%); while 'clothing and footwear' has the lowest rate of growth. High rate of growth being observed in case of education reflects an increasing number of private educational institutions, which charges fees to the students, in urban areas. Private educational institutions have attracted more and more students than governmental institutions even if they charge more fees.

Table 3.5 and 3.6 give the percentage composition of household MPCE corresponding to per capita consumer expenditure (at current prices) given in Table 3.3 and Table 3.4. In both rural and urban areas of the region, the share of food in total expenditure continued to fall throughout the period 1994-95 to 2005-06. The overall fell was from 63.80 per cent to 40.34 per cent in rural areas and from 56.84 per cent to 33.10 per cent in urban areas. The share of cereals and cereals substitutes continuously falls from 28.71 per cent to 13.97 per cent in rural areas and from 22.27 per cent to 8.36 per cent in urban areas during the period under study.

In line with the decreasing share of food items in total expenditure, the share of nonfood items continued to increase from 36.19 per cent in 1993-94 to 59.67 per cent in 2005-06 in rural areas and from 43.16

per cent to 66.88 per cent in urban areas. The share of 'pan, tobacco and intoxicants' group fell noticeably from 8.93 per cent to 3.54 per cent in rural areas and from 4.62 per cent to 2.92 per cent in urban areas. At the same time, other groups of nonfood items—'fuel and light', 'clothing and footwear', and education—do not show any clear pattern.

So far, we have considered only the changes in per capita consumer expenditure for current prices. However, the changes may be due to increases in prices; if so, it will not reflect the real increase in per capita expenditure. To measure the real increase in consumer expenditure we worked out the data in constant price terms using 1993-94 prices as base year. The wholesale price indices provided by Economic Advisory Council, Ministry of Industry, are used to deflate the current price data in order to convert it into constant price term.

The expenditure on total food items at constant price increased from Rs. 216.14 in 1994-95 to Rs. 223.30 in rural areas and from Rs. 250.27 to Rs. 317.82 in urban areas of NER. At the same time, the expenditure (at constant price) on food group of 'cereals and cereals substitutes' is found to decline with compound annual rate of decay of –2.5 per cent in rural areas and –1.52 per cent in urban areas. With the exception of education, per capita expenditure on all other commodity groups, at constant price, has increased considerably during the 10 years study period. The nonfood expenditure recorded the highest rate of increase; it increased from Rs. 113.57 in 1994-95 to Rs. 360.13 in 2005-06 with CAGR of 8.51 in rural areas and from Rs. 176.03 to Rs. 700.17 with CAGR of 10.19 per cent in urban areas. Within nonfood the item group, 'clothing and footwear' recorded the highest rate of growth (i.e. 8.3%) in rural areas; while 'fuel and light being the highest' (i.e. 7.67%) in urban areas of NER.

Corresponding to the component of MPCE at constant price given in Table 3.7 and Table 3.8, we worked the percentage distribution of per capita consumer expenditure in North Eastern Region (NER) in Table 3.9 and 3.10. It has also been observed, in case of constant price term, the share of food items in total expenditure decreased continuously in both rural and urban areas; while the share of nonfood increased in both rural and urban areas. As it has been observed in case of current prices, the share of commodity groups 'pan, tobacco and intoxicants' and 'cereals and cereals substitutes' are found to decline in both rural and urban areas; whereas the share of other groups under consideration do not show any clear pattern.

**Table 3.7:** Average Monthly Expenditure (Rs) Per Person in Rural Areas of North-Eastern India at Constant Price (1993-94=100)

| *Year* | *NSS Round* | *Cereals and Cereals Substitutes* | *Food Total* | *Pan, Tobacco and Intoxicants* | *Fuel and Light* | *Clothing and Footwear* | *Education* | *Nonfood Total* | *Total Consumer Expenditure* |
|---|---|---|---|---|---|---|---|---|---|
| 1994-95 | 51 | 96.90 | 216.14 | 28.03 | 32.87 | 11.23 | 7.85 | 113.57 | 329.72 |
| 1995-96 | 52 | 96.29 | 208.63 | 14.99 | 22.90 | 28.35 | 13.96 | 115.73 | 324.36 |
| 1998 | 54 | 92.01 | 188.66 | 14.90 | 25.18 | 18.69 | 23.44 | 121.96 | 310.62 |
| 1999-00 | 55 | 87.47 | 223.42 | 22.75 | 36.73 | 32.83 | 13.07 | 169.64 | 393.06 |
| 2000-01 | 56 | 92.33 | 215.33 | 19.47 | 37.65 | 34.80 | 16.74 | 172.51 | 387.84 |
| 2001-02 | 57 | 87.34 | 196.87 | 16.54 | 31.53 | 34.35 | 17.79 | 167.94 | 364.81 |
| 2002 | 58 | 81.81 | 197.33 | 19.67 | 36.77 | 37.81 | 16.11 | 173.58 | 370.91 |
| 2003 | 59 | 79.72 | 201.76 | 16.81 | 33.23 | 33.55 | 2.45 | 163.08 | 364.84 |
| 2004 | 60 | 76.38 | 238.30 | 22.48 | 29.98 | 25.63 | 12.92 | 145.38 | 383.68 |
| 2005-06 | 62 | 81.27 | 223.30 | 21.35 | 47.88 | 36.19 | 16.34 | 360.13 | 583.43 |
| CGR (%) | | (-) 2.5 | 0.67 | 0.24 | 4.01 | 8.3 | (-) 2.72 | 8.51 | 4.26 |

**Table 3.8:** Average Monthly Expenditure (Rs) Per Person in Urban Areas of North-Eastern India at Constant Price (1993-94=100)

| *Year* | *NSS Round* | *Cereals and Cereals Substitutes* | *Food Total* | *Pan, Tobacco and Intoxicants* | *Fuel and Light* | *Clothing and Footwears* | *Education* | *Nonfood Total* | *Total Consumer Expenditure* |
|---|---|---|---|---|---|---|---|---|---|
| 1994-95 | 51 | 97.73 | 250.27 | 18.82 | 31.58 | 35.76 | 21.49 | 176.03 | 426.30 |
| 1995-96 | 52 | 95.60 | 257.95 | 21.27 | 30.76 | 39.73 | 32.70 | 214.36 | 472.31 |
| 1998 | 54 | 93.49 | 234.70 | 17.52 | 31.46 | 22.72 | 48.05 | 221.25 | 455.96 |
| 1999-00 | 55 | 88.98 | 288.01 | 28.34 | 42.33 | 48.46 | 30.88 | 308.37 | 596.38 |
| 2000-01 | 56 | 99.95 | 285.54 | 24.33 | 53.87 | 57.26 | 41.38 | 342.33 | 627.86 |
| 2001-02 | 57 | 89.47 | 259.78 | 23.19 | 50.50 | 58.41 | 40.82 | 346.84 | 606.63 |
| 2002 | 58 | 89.42 | 278.28 | 27.36 | 56.24 | 63.90 | 39.16 | 360.62 | 638.91 |
| 2003 | 59 | 85.03 | 261.09 | 18.32 | 47.03 | 49.52 | 3.78 | 293.79 | 554.88 |
| 2004 | 60 | 87.32 | 328.58 | 23.90 | 43.09 | 39.01 | 32.54 | 272.76 | 601.34 |
| 2005-06 | 62 | 84.39 | 317.82 | 30.78 | 69.01 | 57.96 | 42.37 | 700.17 | 1017.99 |
| CGR (%) | | (–) 1.52 | 2.56 | 3.27 | 7.67 | 5.58 | (–) 3.5 | 10.19 | 6.68 |

**Table 3.9:** Percentage Distribution of Total Consumer Expenditure Per Person Per Month Over Groups of Items of Consumption for Rural Areas of North-Eastern India at Constant Price (1993-94=100)

| *Year* | *NSS Round* | *Cereals and Cereals Substitutes* | *Food Total* | *Pan, Tobacco and Intoxicants* | *Fuel and Light* | *Clothing and Footwear* | *Education* | *Nonfood Total* | *Total Consumer Expenditure* |
|---|---|---|---|---|---|---|---|---|---|
| 1994-95 | 51 | 29.39 | 65.55 | 8.50 | 9.97 | 3.40 | 2.38 | 34.45 | 100.00 |
| 1995-96 | 52 | 29.69 | 64.32 | 4.62 | 7.06 | 8.74 | 4.30 | 35.68 | 100.00 |
| 1998 | 54 | 29.62 | 60.74 | 4.80 | 8.11 | 6.02 | 7.54 | 39.26 | 100.00 |
| 1999-00 | 55 | 22.26 | 56.84 | 5.79 | 9.35 | 8.35 | 3.33 | 43.16 | 100.00 |
| 2000-01 | 56 | 23.81 | 55.52 | 5.02 | 9.71 | 8.97 | 4.32 | 44.48 | 100.00 |
| 2001-02 | 57 | 23.94 | 53.97 | 4.53 | 8.64 | 9.42 | 4.88 | 46.03 | 100.00 |
| 2002 | 58 | 22.06 | 53.20 | 5.30 | 9.91 | 10.19 | 4.34 | 46.80 | 100.00 |
| 2003 | 59 | 21.85 | 55.30 | 4.61 | 9.11 | 9.20 | 0.67 | 44.70 | 100.00 |
| 2004 | 60 | 19.91 | 62.11 | 5.86 | 7.81 | 6.68 | 3.37 | 37.89 | 100.00 |
| 2005-06 | 62 | 13.93 | 38.27 | 3.66 | 8.21 | 6.20 | 2.80 | 61.73 | 100.00 |

**Table 3.10:** Percentage Distribution of Total Consumer Expenditure Per Person Per Month Over Groups of Items of Consumption for Urban Areas of North-Eastern India at Constant Price (1993-94=100)

| *Year* | *NSS Round* | *Cereals and Cereals Substitutes* | *Food Total* | *Pan, Tobacco and Intoxicants* | *FUEL and lIght* | *Clothing and Footwears* | *Education* | *Nonfood Total* | *Total Consumer Expenditure* |
|---|---|---|---|---|---|---|---|---|---|
| 1994-95 | 51 | 22.92 | 58.71 | 4.42 | 7.41 | 8.39 | 5.04 | 41.29 | 100.00 |
| 1995-96 | 52 | 20.24 | 54.61 | 4.50 | 6.51 | 8.41 | 6.92 | 45.39 | 100.00 |
| 1998 | 54 | 20.50 | 51.47 | 3.84 | 6.90 | 4.98 | 10.54 | 48.53 | 100.00 |
| 1999-00 | 55 | 14.92 | 48.29 | 4.75 | 7.10 | 8.13 | 5.18 | 51.71 | 100.00 |
| 2000-01 | 56 | 15.92 | 45.48 | 3.87 | 8.58 | 9.12 | 6.59 | 54.52 | 100.00 |
| 2001-02 | 57 | 14.75 | 42.82 | 3.82 | 8.32 | 9.63 | 6.73 | 57.18 | 100.00 |
| 2002 | 58 | 14.00 | 43.56 | 4.28 | 8.80 | 10.00 | 6.13 | 56.44 | 100.00 |
| 2003 | 59 | 15.32 | 47.05 | 3.30 | 8.48 | 8.92 | 0.68 | 52.95 | 100.00 |
| 2004 | 60 | 14.52 | 54.64 | 3.97 | 7.17 | 6.49 | 5.41 | 45.36 | 100.00 |
| 2005-06 | 62 | 8.29 | 31.22 | 3.02 | 6.78 | 5.69 | 4.16 | 68.78 | 100.00 |

## 3.3 INTER-STATE ANALYSIS OF EXPENDITURE PATTERNS IN NER

To study the general pattern of consumer expenditure among 8 states of North-Eastern Region (NER), we had tabulated the ungroup data of the 62nd NSS Round covering the period 2005-06 for the entire region. The analysis of group-wise consumption expenditure will reflect the level of standard of living attained by the society in various states of the region. The details of group-wise per capita consumption expenditure on 13 groups in both rural and urban areas for all states of NER are given in Table 3.11 and the percentage break-up of the total consumption has also given Table 3.12.

The urban monthly per capita consumer expenditure (MPCE) is found to be higher than the MPCE of rural areas in all states of the region. The MPCE of rural areas ranged from Rs. 753 in Tripura, followed by Sikkim which has Rs. 889.2, to Rs. 1728 in Nagaland, followed by Mizoram (Rs. 1340). Urban MPCE ranged from Rs. 1081 in Manipur, followed by Arunachal Pradesh (Rs. 1607), to Rs. 3158 in Nagaland, followed by Mizoram (Rs. 2033). The rural average family size is found to be higher than the average family sizes in urban areas in all States of NER. Average family size in rural areas ranged from 4.83 in Sikkim to 5.46 in Mizoram; while urban average family size ranged from 3.25 in Sikkim to 4.91 in Mizoram.

Table 3.12 gives the percentage composition of household MPCE corresponding to per capita consumer expenditure given in Table 3.11. The share of food items in total consumer expenditure in rural areas is higher than in urban areas for all states. In rural areas, the share of food items is found to be lowest in Nagaland (35.2%) which has highest MPCE; while Tripura, which has the lowest MPCE among the states of NER, has the highest percentage share of food expenditure (47.8). This result reflects the operational evidence of Engel's law of declining food share as income increases. Within food items, in case of 'cereals and cereals substitutes', 'egg, fish and meat' and vegetables the percentage share are found to be higher in rural areas than in urban areas in all states of NER. However, the reverse trend is observed in case of 'milk and milk products' which has higher share in urban areas than rural areas for all states. So, the consumption of this item group is more dependent on the income of the households than all other food items. At the same time, the percentage share of 'other food items' does not show any clear pattern.

**Table 3.11:** Average Monthly Per Capita Consumer Expenditure (in Rs.) on Item Groups in the States of North-Eastern Region on the 62nd NSS Round (2005-06)

| *Item Groups* | *AP* | | *Assam* | | *Manipur* | | *Meghalaya* | | *Mizoram* | |
|---|---|---|---|---|---|---|---|---|---|---|
| | *R* | *U* | *R* | *U* | *R* | *U* | *R* | *U* | *R* | *U* |
| Cereals and cereal substitutes | 168.6 | 146 | 142 | 140.6 | 206 | 200 | 133.51 | 132.8 | 143 | 159 |
| **Milk and milk products** | **26.98** | **57.9** | **30.09** | **57.31** | **8.31** | **17.7** | **16.26** | **34.72** | **21.7** | **56.2** |
| Egg, fish and meat | 93.85 | 112 | 72.2 | 96.87 | 51.2 | 64.4 | 95.76 | 117.1 | 91.7 | 134 |
| **Vegetables** | **67.49** | **75.5** | **63.32** | **79.55** | **37.8** | **45.5** | **63.61** | **74.79** | **102** | **125** |
| Other food items | 113.3 | 154 | 119.5 | 293 | 83.1 | 118 | 120.8 | 220.7 | 135 | 169 |
| **Food total** | **470.3** | **546** | **427.1** | **667.4** | **386** | **445** | **429.94** | **580** | **493** | **643** |
| Pan, tobacco and intoxicants | 63.75 | 44.4 | 26.66 | 47.28 | 20.1 | 23.7 | 59.08 | 94.86 | 45 | 85.5 |
| Fuel and light | 128.6 | 114 | 71.94 | 127 | 93.3 | 108 | 74.2 | 122.6 | 99.1 | 125 |
| **Clothing, bedding and footwear** | **64.93** | **104** | **54.33** | **90.93** | **42.3** | **47.2** | **73.51** | **112.8** | **106** | **158** |
| Education | 17.06 | 31 | 18.7 | 66.36 | 46.5 | 53.3 | 28.69 | 119.3 | 24.9 | 67.6 |
| Medical | 22.49 | 30.1 | 17.93 | 47.71 | 18.1 | 20.5 | 15.29 | 35.18 | 21.1 | 37 |
| **Durables** | **180.3** | **475** | **396.9** | **510.9** | **222** | **204** | **256.81** | **173.8** | **371** | **472** |
| Other nonfood items | 172.4 | 262 | 96.82 | 435.8 | 129 | 180 | 137.32 | 514.5 | 181 | 444 |
| **Non-food total** | **649.6** | **1061** | **683.3** | **1326** | **571** | **636** | **644.9** | **1173** | **847** | **1390** |
| MPCE | 1120 | 1607 | 1110 | 1994 | 957 | 1081 | 1074.9 | 1753 | 1340 | 2033 |
| Average household size | 5.09 | 3.59 | 5.5 | 3.89 | 5.46 | 5.27 | 5.27 | 4.35 | 5.46 | 4.91 |

**Table 3.11 (*Contd.*)**

| *Item groups* | *Nagaland* | | *Sikkim* | | *Tripura* | | *NER* | |
|---|---|---|---|---|---|---|---|---|
| | *R* | *U* | *R* | *U* | *R* | *U* | *R* | *U* |
| Cereals and cereal substitutes | 185.5 | 189 | 116 | 127.9 | 128 | 163 | 150.97 | 156.8 |
| **Milk and milk products** | **45** | **75.3** | **60.31** | **76.95** | **24.2** | **64.7** | 27.304 | 54.53 |
| Egg, fish and meat | 158.6 | 192 | 51.25 | 68.15 | 71.8 | 131 | 83.035 | 114.3 |
| **Vegetables** | **88.32** | **111** | **70.13** | **81.91** | **53.9** | **78.4** | 64.857 | 84.4 |
| Other food items | 131 | 241 | 120.4 | 313.9 | 81.8 | 156 | 109.96 | 210.7 |
| **Food total** | **608.4** | **809** | **418.1** | **668.8** | **360** | **593** | **436.12** | **620.7** |
| Pan, tobacco and intoxicants | 55.36 | 71.7 | 25.73 | 45.9 | 27.3 | 38.7 | 38.238 | 55.13 |
| Fuel and light | 123.2 | 157 | 82.7 | 111.1 | 55.1 | 120 | 85.746 | 123.6 |
| **Clothing, bedding and footwear** | **95.81** | **128** | **94.77** | **149** | **46.7** | **84** | 64.808 | 103.8 |
| Education | 86.14 | 145 | 21.08 | 54.16 | 20.4 | 78.4 | 29.267 | 75.88 |
| Medical | 20.92 | 30.2 | 7.57 | 18.15 | 30.8 | 102 | 20.616 | 48.42 |
| **Durables** | **495.4** | **1189** | **88.21** | **129** | **114** | **287** | **269.46** | **426.1** |
| Other nonfood items | 243.2 | 627 | 151 | 672.7 | 98.1 | 372 | 136.83 | 421.4 |
| **Non-food total** | **1120** | **2348** | **471.1** | **1180** | **393** | **1081** | **644.96** | **1254** |
| Mpce | 1728 | 3156 | 889.2 | 1849 | 753 | 1674 | 1081.1 | 1875 |
| Average household size | 5.22 | 4.41 | 4.83 | 3.25 | 4.89 | 3.76 | 5.2 | 4.2 |

**Table 3.12:** Percentage Break-up Consumer Expenditure on the 62nd NSS Round (2005-06) in North-Eastern India

| *Item Groups* | *AP* | | *Assam* | | *Manipur* | | *Meghalaya* | | *Mizoram* | |
|---|---|---|---|---|---|---|---|---|---|---|
| | *R* | *U* | *R* | *U* | *R* | *U* | *R* | *U* | *R* | *U* |
| Cereals and cereal substitutes | 15.1 | 9.1 | 12.8 | 7.1 | 21.5 | 18.5 | 12.4 | 7.6 | 10.6 | 7.8 |
| **Milk and milk products** | **2.4** | **3.6** | **2.7** | **2.9** | **0.9** | **1.6** | **1.5** | **2.0** | **1.6** | **2.8** |
| Egg, fish and meat | 8.4 | 7.0 | 6.5 | 4.9 | 5.4 | 6.0 | 8.9 | 6.7 | 6.8 | 6.6 |
| **Vegetables** | **6.0** | **4.7** | **5.7** | **4.0** | **4.0** | **4.2** | **5.9** | **4.3** | **7.6** | **6.2** |
| Other food items | 10.1 | 9.6 | 10.8 | 14.7 | 8.7 | 10.9 | 11.2 | 12.6 | 10.1 | 8.3 |
| **Food total** | **42.0** | **34.0** | **38.5** | **33.5** | **40.3** | **41.2** | **40.0** | **33.1** | **36.8** | **31.6** |
| Pan, tobacco and intoxicants | 5.7 | 2.8 | 2.4 | 2.4 | 2.1 | 2.2 | 5.5 | 5.4 | 3.4 | 4.2 |
| Fuel and light | 11.5 | 7.1 | 6.5 | 6.4 | 9.8 | 10.0 | 6.9 | 7.0 | 7.4 | 6.2 |
| **Clothing, bedding and footwear** | **5.8** | **6.5** | **4.9** | **4.6** | **4.4** | **4.4** | **6.8** | **6.4** | **7.9** | **7.8** |
| Education | 1.5 | 1.9 | 1.7 | 3.3 | 4.9 | 4.9 | 2.7 | 6.8 | 1.9 | 3.3 |
| Medical | 2.0 | 1.9 | 1.6 | 2.4 | 1.9 | 1.9 | 1.4 | 2.0 | 1.6 | 1.8 |
| **Durables** | **16.1** | **29.6** | **35.8** | **25.6** | **23.2** | **18.9** | **23.9** | **9.9** | **27.7** | **23.2** |
| Other nonfood items | 15.4 | 16.3 | 8.7 | 21.9 | 13.5 | 16.6 | 12.8 | 29.3 | 13.5 | 21.9 |
| **Non-food total** | **58.0** | **66.0** | **61.6** | **66.5** | **59.7** | **58.8** | **60.0** | **66.9** | **63.2** | **68.4** |

**Table 3.12 (*Contd.*)**

| *Item Groups* | *Nagaland* | | *Sikkim* | | *Tripura* | | *NER* | |
|---|---|---|---|---|---|---|---|---|
| | *R* | *U* | *R* | *U* | *R* | *U* | *R* | *U* |
| Egg, fish and meat | 9.2 | 6.1 | 5.8 | 3.7 | 9.5 | 7.8 | 7.7 | 6.1 |
| **Vegetables** | **5.1** | **3.5** | **7.9** | **4.4** | **7.2** | **4.7** | **6.0** | **4.5** |
| Other food items | 7.6 | 7.6 | 13.5 | 17.0 | 10.9 | 9.3 | 10.2 | 11.2 |
| **Food total** | **35.2** | **25.6** | **47.0** | **36.2** | **47.8** | **35.4** | **40.3** | **33.1** |
| Pan, tobacco and intoxicants | 3.2 | 2.3 | 2.9 | 2.5 | 3.6 | 2.3 | 3.5 | 2.9 |
| Fuel and light | 7.1 | 5.0 | 9.3 | 6.0 | 7.3 | 7.1 | 7.9 | 6.6 |
| **Clothing, bedding and footwear** | **5.5** | **4.0** | **10.7** | **8.1** | **6.2** | **5.0** | **6.0** | **5.5** |
| Education | 5.0 | 4.6 | 2.4 | 2.9 | 2.7 | 4.7 | 2.7 | 4.0 |
| Medical | 1.2 | 1.0 | 0.9 | 1.0 | 4.1 | 6.1 | 1.9 | 2.6 |
| **Durables** | **28.7** | **37.7** | **9.9** | **7.0** | **15.2** | **17.1** | **24.9** | **22.7** |
| Other nonfood items | 14.1 | 19.9 | 17.0 | 36.4 | 13.0 | 22.2 | 12.7 | 22.5 |
| **Non-food total** | **64.8** | **74.4** | **53.0** | **63.8** | **52.2** | **64.6** | **59.7** | **66.9** |

In rural areas, the percentage share of 'pan, tobacco and intoxicants' group is lowest in Manipur; while it is highest in Arunachal Pradesh. In urban areas, it ranged from 2.2 per cent in Manipur to 4.2 per cent in Mizoram. Thus, share of 'pan, tobacco and intoxicants' in case of both rural and urban areas is observed in Manipur. The percentage share of rural consumption on 'fuel and light' is highest in Arunachal Pradesh; while it is lowest in Nagaland. In urban areas, it is highest in Manipur and lowest in Nagaland. Moreover, the share of 'fuel and lights' in total consumer expenditure is generally high in rural areas.

One of the major components of total consumer expenditure in the region is the group of 'clothing, bedding and footwear'. Its share varies from 4.4 per cent in rural areas of Arunachal Pradesh to 10.7 per cent in rural Sikkim; while in urban areas, it varies from 4 per cent in Nagaland to 8.1 per cent in Sikkim. Further, not much difference between rural and urban areas has been observed in the consumption of 'education' and 'medical' groups.

The largest component of total consumer expenditure among nonfood items in all areas of NER is 'durables' group. Generally, its shares are higher in rural areas than in urban areas in all states except for Arunachal Pradesh, Nagaland and Tripura. In rural areas, it share varies from 9.9 per cent in Sikkim to 35.8 per cent in Assam; while in urban areas, it ranged from 7 per cent in Sikkim to 37.7 per cent in Nagaland.

The share of 'other nonfood items' are considerably high in urban areas. Diversification of consumption can be made more in urban areas than rural areas of NER. The percentage share of rural expenditure on this group ranged from 8.7 per cent in Assam to 17 per cent in Sikkim; while in urban areas, it ranged from 16.3 per cent in Arunachal Pradesh to 36.4 per cent in Sikkim.

The share of nonfood items in total consumer expenditure is higher in urban areas than in rural areas for all states of NER. This corresponds to the decreasing share of food consumption with the increase in income or total consumer expenditure. It also reflects the weak purchasing power of rural community in the region. Further, the present analysis revealed food accounted for more than one-third of the total consumer expenditure in North-Eastern India implying the low standard of living of the people as compared to the advanced countries which spend less than one-fourth on food items[7].

## 3.4 PATTERN OF CONSUMER EXPENDITURE IN MIZORAM BASED ON THE PRIMARY DATA

In addition to the above analysis of the pattern of consumer expenditure based on the 62nd NSS Rounds, we carried out a study on the pattern of consumer expenditure based on our sample survey conducted during July-August, 2007. This survey covered 372 households, 193 urban household and 179 rural households, in Mizoram. The finding are tabulated and presented in Table 3.13 and Table 3.14.

Table 3.13 presents the expenditure pattern of Mizoram obtained from our sample survey conducted during July-August, 2007. Broadly the per capita consumer expenditure on all groups of items is higher in urban areas than in rural areas. Monthly Per Capita Consumer Expenditure (MPCE) in urban areas is Rs. 2731.82, which is more than two times the per capita monthly consumer expenditure in rural areas, which is Rs. 1151.26. The MPCE of Mizoram is Rs. 1971.28 against the per capita monthly income (PMI) of Rs. 2414.76 indicating the average propensity to consume is 0.82. In line with the differences in MPCE between rural and urban areas, per capita monthly income of urban areas is Rs. 3506.66 against Rs. 1237.46 in rural areas. The PMI of urban areas is almost three times the PMI of rural areas. On the basis of this estimate, the average propensity to consume works out to be 0.93 in rural areas and 0.78 in urban areas, which indicates that as income increases average propensity to consume (ratio of consumption to income) decreases as stated in the Keynesian Absolute Income Hypothesis.

The main factor causing the differences in consumption expenditure between rural and urban areas may be attributable to the following: first, the cost of living is much higher in urban areas than in rural areas; second, the consumption of non-food items including luxury items increases at an accelerated rate as income increases. The ratio of food to non-food item is 0.57 in rural areas and 0.37 in urban areas indicating that there is a tendency to consume luxury items as income level increases. Finally, under-valuation of own-produced consumption leads to understatement of per capita consumption in rural areas. In rural areas, the majority of food items consumed are own-produced. In the process of valuation of such items the possibility of under-valuation is very high.

The monthly per capita consumer expenditure of Mizoram on food items is Rs. 578.15. Within the food items considered in the field survey, the amounts spent on the item group of 'cereals, salt, sugar and edible oils' was found to be the highest followed by beverages. It was Rs. 177.96

for 'cereals, salt, sugar and edible oils' and Rs. 141.24 beverages respectively. The per capita expenditure was found to be the lowest in case of meat item that is Rs. 122.84.

Significant difference on the amount of spending on food items is observed between rural and urban areas. For all the food groups under considerations, urban average spending range between Rs. 150 and Rs. 205; while in the rural areas, it is within Rs. 70 and Rs. 160. In case of the items of beverages and meat, urban spending are more than two times the rural spending. Average spending on beverages is Rs. 74.78 in rural areas against Rs. 202.88 in urban areas. Similarly, the consumption spending on meat in urban areas averaged to Rs. 167.54 as against Rs. 74.59 in rural areas. In case of 'cereals, salt, sugar and edible oils', the average spending is Rs. 157.62 in rural areas as against Rs. 196.82 in urban areas. The average expenditure on vegetables is Rs. 108.39 in rural areas while it is Rs. 196.82 in urban areas. It is observed in all food items that average expenditure in rural areas is below the State's averages and that of the urban areas is above it.

**Table 3.13:** Average Expenditure (Rs) Per Person Per Month on Selected Groups of Items of Consumption

| *Sl No* | *Items* | *Average Expenditure (in Rs)* | | |
|---|---|---|---|---|
| | | *Rural* | *Urban* | *Mizoram* |
| 1. | Beverages | 74.78 | 202.88 | 141.24 |
| 2. | Meat | 74.59 | 167.59 | 122.84 |
| 3. | Vegetables | 108.39 | 161.84 | 136.12 |
| 4. | Cereals, salt, sugar and edible oils | 157.62 | 196.82 | 177.96 |
| **5.** | **Food item** | **415.38** | **729.11** | **578.15** |
| 6. | Pan, tobacco and intoxicants | 101.12 | 142.31 | 122.49 |
| 7. | Entertainment and telecommunications | 93.49 | 248.84 | 174.09 |
| 8. | Health care | 57.44 | 89.5 | 74.07 |
| 9. | Clothing and housing | 231.25 | 583.39 | 413.94 |
| 10. | Education | 98.57 | 300.53 | 203.35 |
| 11. | Transportations | 38.03 | 96.76 | 68.5 |
| 12. | Miscellaneous | 115.98 | 541.39 | 336.69 |
| **13.** | **Non food item** | **735.88** | **2002.71** | **1393.13** |
| **14.** | **Monthly per capita consumer expenditure (MPCE)** | **1151.26** | **2731.82** | **1971.28** |
| 15. | Per capita monthly income | 1237.46 | 3506.66 | 2414.76 |

*Source*: Sample Survey: July-August, 2007.

Per capita consumption expenditure on non-foods items in Mizoram is Rs. 1393.13. Among the non-food items under study, the amount spent on 'clothing and housing' is the highest followed by miscellaneous items, education and 'entertainments and telecommunications'. This is found to be Rs. 413.94 for clothing and housing, Rs. 336.69 for miscellaneous items, Rs. 203.35 for education and Rs. 174.09 for 'entertainment and telecommunications'. The lowest figure is observed in transportations (Rs. 68.5) followed by health care (Rs. 74.07).

The lowest rural-urban difference in the amount of per capita expenditure was found in case of health care followed by 'pan, tobacco and intoxicants'. In case of health care, it is Rs. 57.44 and Rs. 89.5 for rural and urban areas respectively. Similarly for the items group of 'pan, tobacco and intoxicants', the variations in the rates of per capita expenditure are Rs. 101.12 and Rs. 142.31 for rural and urban areas respectively. On the other hand, the highest difference of per capita expenditure between rural and urban areas is on miscellaneous items followed by education. Per capita expenditure on miscellaneous items in urban areas is Rs. 541.39 that is almost as high as five times the average expenditure on miscellaneous items in rural areas (Rs. 115.980). For education, the average expenditure, which is found to be Rs. 300.53 in urban areas, is more than three times the average rural expenditure, which stands at Rs. 98.57. The overall difference in the amount of per capita expenditure between rural and urban areas is higher in non-food items than in food items. This is due to the fact that food is necessity whose consumption hardly increase with the increase in income; whereas, the consumption of non-food items increases with the levels of income.

The detail of percentage break-up of various commodity groups is presented in Table 3.14 and Figure 3.3 below. Food expenditure accounts for 29.3 per cent, while non-food accounts for 70.67 per cent. The share of 'cereals, salt, sugar and edible oils' is the largest among the food items and the share of meat is found to be the smallest. 'Clothing and housing' took the largest share (21%) for all items followed by miscellaneous items (17.08%). The share of transportation at 3.47 per cent is the smallest followed by health care (3.76%).

Thus the analysis of the data reveals that there is a wide disparity of consumption patterns between rural and urban areas. In rural areas, the percent of food expenditure is 36.08 against 26.69 per cent in urban areas. Since the per capita monthly consumer expenditure in urban areas is higher than in rural areas, the given data supports the proposition of the theory of decreasing proportion of food consumption with the increase in

**Table 3.14:** Percentage Distribution of Total Consumer Expenditure Per Person Per Month Over Selected Groups of Items

| *Sl. No* | *Items* | *Percentage share* | | |
|---|---|---|---|---|
| | | *Rural* | *Urban* | *Both Areas* |
| 1. | Beverages | 6.5 | 7.43 | 7.16 |
| 2. | Meat | 6.48 | 6.13 | 6.23 |
| 3. | Vegetables | 9.41 | 5.92 | 6.91 |
| 4. | Cereals, salt, sugar and edible oils | 13.69 | 7.2 | 9.03 |
| **5.** | **Food item** | **36.08** | **26.69** | **29.33** |
| 6. | Pan and tobacco and its products | 8.78 | 5.21 | 6.21 |
| 7. | Entertainment and telecommunications | 8.12 | 9.11 | 8.83 |
| 8. | Health Care | 4.99 | 3.28 | 3.76 |
| 9. | Clothing and housing | 20.08 | 21.36 | 21 |
| 10. | Education | 8.56 | 11 | 10.32 |
| 11. | Transportations | 3.3 | 3.54 | 3.47 |
| 12. | Miscellaneous | 10.07 | 19.82 | 17.08 |
| **13.** | **Non-food Item** | **63.92** | **73.31** | **70.67** |
| **14.** | **Monthly per capita consumer expenditure** | 100 | 100 | 100 |

*Source*: Sample Survey: July-August, 2007.

consumption expenditure. Among the food items, the share group of 'cereals, salt, sugar and edible oils' accounts for the largest (13.69%) in rural areas whereas beverages (7.43%) accounts for the largest in urban areas. There is only marginal difference between rural and urban areas in the share of meat consumption. It is 6.48 per cent in rural areas and 6.13 per cent in urban areas. The share of vegetables in rural areas is 9.41 per cent, which is significantly higher than 5.92 per cent in urban areas.

Except for miscellaneous items, rural and urban areas show more or less the same pattern of consumption in non-food items. 'Clothing and housing' accounts for the largest share both in rural and urban areas. They are 20.08 per cent and 21.36 per cent for rural and urban areas respectively. Miscellaneous items take 10.07 per cent in rural areas against 19.82 per cent in urban areas. It may be argued that the greater diversity of consumption items in urban areas than in rural areas leads to wide disparity in the consumption of miscellaneous items. In rural areas, 'pan, tobacco and intoxicants' accounts for 8.78 per cent while in urban areas it is 5.21 per cent. Since these items are addictive in nature, the amount spent on these items is normally the same irrespective of whether the consumer's income is low or high. This led to the high share in rural areas even though the absolute amount of expenditure is low. For the commodity groups of entertainment and telecommunications, health care, education and transportations the percentage share are almost same for rural and urban areas.

## 3.5 PATTERN OF EXPENDITURE AMONG VARIOUS MPCE CLASSES

Since private final consumption expenditure is a direct measure of the living standard of the people, an analysis of the pattern of consumption expenditure on groups of items for different MPCE classes would highlight the living standard of the people in each class and; at the same time it represented the inequality of consumption among the people. In Table 3.15 is presented the average per person expenditure on group of items for various MPCE classes. The average MPCE is Rs. 534.94 in the lowest group (Rs. 0-840) and it is Rs. 5639.77 in the highest group (Rs. 4200-+). This implies that the average consumption of the highest MPCE group is more than 10 times the total average consumption of the lowest MPCE group. Therefore, this is a clear indication that there is wide disparity in terms of consumption among the people in the state as the range of PMCE is Rs. 5104.83. It is also observed that with the increase in MPCE there is a tendency for the average family size to decrease.

The amount spent on food items increase from Rs. 295.83 in Rs. 0-840 MPCE class to Rs. 840.18 in Rs. 4200-+ MPCE class, which indicates the range of food consumption, is Rs. 544.35. At the same time, the amount spent on non-food items increase from Rs. 239.11 in Rs. 0-840 MPCE class to Rs. 4799.59 in Rs. 4200-+ class indicating that the range of non-food consumption is Rs. 4560.48. Hence, the level of inequality in consumption is much higher in non-food items than in food items. Food consumption is more or less consistent in comparison with the consumption of non-food items.

Within the food items, the items group of cereals, salt, sugar and edible oils shows the lowest degree of consumption inequality as the value of its range is Rs. 73.75; whereas beverages shows the highest consumption inequality as the value of its range is Rs. 249.61. The item group of clothing and housing shows the highest consumption inequality among the non-food items. The range of per capita consumption on clothing and housing is Rs. 1416.61. At the same time, the items group of 'pan, tobacco and intoxicants' shows the lowest consumption inequality among the non-food items.

**Table 3.15:** Average Per Person Consumption Expenditure on Group of Items for Different PMCE Classes

| *Items* | *MPCE (Rs.) Classes* | | | | | | |
|---|---|---|---|---|---|---|---|
| | 0-840 | 840-1680 | 840-2520 | 2520-3360 | 3360-4200 | 4200-+ | *All Classes* |
| Beverages | 29.49 | 101.35 | 189.57 | 223.67 | 279.1 | 270.89 | 141.24 |
| Meat | 43.65 | 107.96 | 161.61 | 174.64 | 199.73 | 192.17 | 122.84 |
| Vegetables | 76.2 | 105.71 | 158.71 | 194.96 | 224.18 | 205.89 | 136.12 |
| Cereals, salt, sugar and edible oils | 146.49 | 170.88 | 202.75 | 204.34 | 219.75 | 171.23 | 177.96 |
| **Food item** | **295.83** | **485.89** | **712.65** | **797.62** | **922.77** | **840.18** | **578.15** |
| Pan, tobacco and intoxicants | 63.25 | 106.14 | 145.74 | 154.28 | 180.25 | 214.5 | 122.49 |
| Entertainment and telecommunications | 19.96 | 114.63 | 198.92 | 274.15 | 367.13 | 459.02 | 174.09 |
| Health care | 14.96 | 53.98 | 101.28 | 111.18 | 110.88 | 179.44 | 74.07 |
| Clothing and housing | 38.29 | 139.61 | 394.33 | 750.49 | 973.74 | 1454.9 | 413.94 |
| Education | 33.01 | 88.1 | 195.5 | 291.56 | 406.68 | 757.05 | 203.35 |
| Transportations | 12.19 | 34.95 | 53.07 | 82.46 | 106.92 | 317.46 | 68.5 |
| Miscellaneous Items | 57.45 | 167.94 | 267.17 | 429.88 | 651.62 | 1417.3 | 336.69 |
| **Non-food Item** | **239.11** | **705.35** | **1356** | **2094** | **2797.2** | **4799.6** | **1393.13** |
| **MPCE** | **534.94** | **1191.3** | **2068.7** | **2891.62** | **3719.98** | **5639.8** | **1971.28** |
| PMI | 563.97 | 1321.6 | 2499.5 | 3310.91 | 3377.78 | 8980.9 | 2414.76 |
| No. of families | 100 | 100 | 64 | 45 | 29 | 33 | 372 |
| Average family size | 6.1 | 6.4 | 6.1 | 5.2 | 5.4 | 5.2 | 5.9 |

*Source*: Sample Survey, July-August, 2007.

At a given level of per capita income/total expenditure the Engel ratios, i.e. proportions of total expenditure spent on various items to total expenditure, provide a broad picture of consumption pattern (Coondoo, 1975)[8]. To examine the consumption pattern of various classes, the researcher works out the movement of Engel ratios for various commodity groups for each of the MPCE class. Table 3.16 presents the item-wise Engel ratios in percentage terms.

As it is depicted in the above table, the percentage share of food decreased with the increase in total expenditure. It decreases from 55.3 per cent in Rs. 0-840 class to 40.79 per cent in Rs. 840-1680 class to 14.9 per cent in Rs. 4200-+ classes. For the broad groups of our survey data, there is a tendency for Engel's ratio to decrease as total expenditures increase, which is in conformity with Engel's Law. The decline in the share of food items is presented in Figure 3.3. Among the food items, there is a sharp decrease in the percentage share of cereals, salt, sugar and edible oils which decrease from 27.38 per cent in the lowest MPCE class to 3.04 per cent in the highest MPCE class; whereas the share of beverages has an increasing tendency up to Rs. 3360-4200 PMCE class. It may be reasonable to infer that the item group of cereals, salt, sugar and edible oils is the most inelastic that consist the staple food and at the same time beverage is the most elastic items among the foods items considered in the study.

The percentage share of non-food items increases with the increase in the level of total expenditure. It increase from 44.7 per cent in Rs. 0-840 class to 85.1 per cent in Rs. 4200-+ class implying that as total income/ expenditure increases, the percentage share of non-food increases. As a result of which non-food items can be considered as elastic goods. With the exception of 'pan, tobacco and intoxicants', whose percentage share decrease from 11.82 per cent in the lowest MPCE class to 3.8 per cent in the highest MPCE class, the share of non-foods items like 'entertainment and telecommunication', health care, 'clothing and housing', education, transportation, and miscellaneous items increase with the increase in the total expenditure.

## 3.6 CONCENTRATION IN CONSUMER EXPENDITURE

Concentration curves of expenditure can be used to study the degree of concentration in consumer expenditure. The concentration curve gives the percentage 100q of the total consumption expenditure by the poorest 100p per cent of the population (Singh & Singh, 1971)[9]. So the curve is

**Table 3.16:** Percentage Break Up of Per Person Consumption Expenditure on Group of Items for Different PMCE Classes

| *Items* | *PMCE (Rs) Classes* | | | | | | |
|---|---|---|---|---|---|---|---|
| | 0-840 | 840-1680 | 840-2520 | 2520-3360 | 3360-4200 | 4200-+ | *All Classes* |
| Beverages | 5.51 | 8.51 | 9.16 | 7.74 | 7.5 | 4.8 | 7.16 |
| Meat | 8.16 | 9.06 | 7.81 | 6.04 | 5.37 | 3.41 | 6.23 |
| Vegetables | 14.24 | 8.87 | 7.67 | 6.74 | 6.03 | 3.65 | 6.91 |
| Cereals, salt, sugar and edible oils | 27.38 | 14.34 | 9.8 | 7.07 | 5.91 | 3.04 | 9.03 |
| **Food Items** | **55.3** | **40.79** | **34.45** | **27.58** | **24.81** | **14.9** | **29.33** |
| Pan, tobacco and intoxicants | 11.82 | 8.91 | 7.04 | 5.34 | 4.84 | 3.8 | 6.21 |
| Entertainment and telecommunications | 3.73 | 9.62 | 9.62 | 9.48 | 9.87 | 8.14 | 8.83 |
| Health care | 2.8 | 4.53 | 4.89 | 3.84 | 2.98 | 3.18 | 3.76 |
| **Clothing and housing** | **7.16** | **11.72** | **19.06** | **25.95** | **26.18** | **25.8** | **21** |
| Education | 6.17 | 7.39 | 9.45 | 10.08 | 10.93 | 13.42 | 10.32 |
| Transportations | 2.28 | 2.93 | 2.56 | 2.85 | 2.87 | 5.63 | 3.47 |
| Miscellaneous Items | 10.74 | 14.1 | 12.92 | 14.87 | 17.52 | 25.13 | 17.08 |
| **Non-food** | **44.7** | **59.21** | **65.55** | **72.42** | **75.19** | **85.1** | **70.67** |
| MPCE | 100 | 100 | 100 | 100 | 100 | 100 | 100 |
| APC | 0.95 | 0.9 | 0.83 | 0.87 | 1.1 | 0.63 | 0.82 |
| No. of families | 100 | 100 | 64 | 45 | 29 | 33 | 372 |
| Average family size | 6.1 | 6.4 | 6.1 | 5.2 | 5.4 | 5.2 | 5.9 |

*Source*: Sample Survey, July-August, 2007.

absolutely independent of units of money and can readily be used to compare the concentration in consumer expenditure of the rural with the urban areas and also between different groups of commodities.

The survey estimated (Table 3.17) about 53 per cent of the Mizoram rural population belonged to households with monthly per capita expenditure less than Rs. 840 (at 2007 prices). In urban Mizoram, where expenditure levels are higher, nearly 34 per cent of the population belonged to households with monthly per capita expenditure of less than Rs. 1880. In Mizoram, as a whole, 28.2 per cent of the total population belonged to the households with monthly per capita expenditure of less than Rs. 840 at 2007 prices.

Table 3.17 shows that more than half (57.2%) of the total population who are in the lower expenditure group account for less than one-fourth (23.8%) of the total consumer expenditure. At the same time, the upper 14.6 per cent of the population account for more than one-third (40.2%) of the total consumer expenditure. In the consumption of food items, 57.2 per cent of the population accounts for 36.6 per cent of the total consumer expenditure while the top 14.6 per cent of the population accounts for 25.4 per cent of the total expenditure on food items. In regards to the consumption of non-food items, 57.2 per cent of the population in the lower consumption bracket accounts for 18.46 per cent; whereas the 14.6 per cent of the population in the upper MPCE bracket accounts for 46.36 per cent of the total consumer expenditure on non-food items.

It would be observed from the above table that more than half (53.1%) of the people of rural areas who are in the lowest consumption bracket accounts for 36 per cent, 16.4 per cent and 23.43 per cent of the total rural consumer expenditure on food, non-food and total consumer expenditure respectively. At the same time, almost 10 per cent of the rural population who are in the top consumption bracket account for 19 per cent, 38.1 per cent and 31.19 per cent of the total expenditure on food, non-food items and total rural consumer expenditure respectively.

Further, more than half (56.3%) of the urban population who are in the lower consumption bracket account for 47.74 per cent of the total consumer expenditure on food and 26.22 per cent on non-food items; and 31.43 per cent of the total consumer expenditure. At the same time, the top 13.4 per cent of the urban population account for 17.9 per cent of total consumer expenditure on food and 36.06 per cent of non-food items; and 50.51 per cent of the total urban consumer expenditure.

**Table 3.17:** Concentration in Food, Non-Food and Total Consumer Expenditure

| *MPCE (Rs) Classes* | *Cumulative Percent Persons* | | *Cumulative Consumer Expenditure on Food* | | *Cumulative Consumer Expenditure on non-Food* | | *Cumulative Total Consumer Expenditure* | | *All Areas* | | | |
|---|---|---|---|---|---|---|---|---|---|---|---|---|
| | *Rural* | *Urban* | *Rural* | *Urban* | *Rural* | *Urban* | *Rural* | *Urban* | *Cumulative Percent Persons* | *Cumulative% Expenditure on Food* | *Cumulative% Expenditure on Non-Food* | *Cumulative% Total Consumer Expenditure* |
| 0-840 | 53.1 | 4.2 | 36 | 2.3 | 16.4 | 0.73 | 23.4 | 1.1 | 28.2 | 13.9 | 4.7009 | 7.409 |
| 840-1680 | 81.5 | 33.9 | 66.4 | 20.81 | 43.6 | 9.88 | 51.84 | 12.8 | 57.2 | 36.6 | 18.458 | 23.77 |
| 1680-2520 | 90.6 | 59.3 | 81 | 45.74 | 61.9 | 26.2 | 68.81 | 31.43 | 74.5 | 57.9 | 35.294 | 41.94 |
| 2520-3360 | 96.6 | 75.1 | 93.3 | 64.75 | 82.1 | 43.9 | 86.15 | 49.49 | 85.4 | 74.6 | 53.641 | 59.79 |
| 3360-4200 | 98.5 | 86.6 | 97.1 | 81.84 | 90.9 | 62.1 | 93.16 | 67.38 | 92.2 | 87.1 | 69.438 | 74.62 |
| 4200-+ | 100 | 100 | 100 | 100 | 100 | 100 | 100 | 100 | 100 | 100 | 100 | 100 |

*Source*: Based on the Sample Survey 2007.

It is observed that there is more concentration in the consumption of non-food items than in food item for both rural and urban areas. The magnitudes of the concentration are more or less same in each of the food and non-food item for rural and urban areas.

In an attempt to quantify the degree of concentration of consumer expenditure on food and non-food items, the Gini concentration ratio has been calculated as follows:

Let the total frequency of the population be N and let I be the total income. Let

$$p_x = \frac{Number\ of\ persons\ with\ income \leq x}{N}$$

$$q_x = \frac{Total\ income\ of\ persons\ with\ income \leq x}{I}$$

If there is a functional relationship between $p_x$ and $q_x$ for all values of x, we can write

$$q_x = f(p_x) \qquad \ldots (3.1)$$

Gini suggested the functional form to be

$$q_x = 1-(1-p_x)^{1/d} \qquad \ldots (3.2)$$

Therefore, the concentration ratio ($\ell$) is defined as

$$\ell = 1 - 2\int_0^1 q_x(p_x)dp_x$$

$$\ell = \frac{d-1}{d+1} \qquad \ldots (3.3)$$

**Table 3.18:** Lorenz Concentration Ratios for Food, Non-Food and Total Consumer Expenditure in Mizoram

| *Items* | *Lorenz Concentration Ratios* | | |
|---|---|---|---|
| | *Rural* | *Urban* | *All Areas* |
| Food Items | 0.2 | 0.16 | 0.22 |
| Non-Food Items | 0.42 | 0.42 | 0.46 |
| Total Consumer Expenditure (PMCE) | 0.34 | 0.35 | 0.39 |

*Source*: Sample Survey, July-August, 2007.

In the Table 3.18 above is presented the concentration ratios for food, non-food and total consumer expenditure. The concentration ratios for food, non-food and total consumer expenditure are higher in all cases as we take the whole areas under study. It would be observed from the table that: (1) the concentration in case of food items is higher in rural areas than in urban areas; (2) the concentration ratios in case of non-food items are same for both rural and urban areas; (3) higher degree of concentration is observed in urban areas in case of total consumer expenditure than in rural areas; and (4) there is more concentration in case of non-food items than in food items.

## Concluding Remarks

The preceding analysis has revealed that all the measures that have been employed to ascertain the pattern of consumer behaviour in the study area do support our hypotheses. It has been found from the result of this statistical analysis that the household expenditure on food increased proportionately less than the increase in income. On examining the various income classes and the proportion of their expenditure on food, we have also shown the falling share of food in percentage terms as income rises. At the same time, it has also been indicated that the average propensity to consume is relatively higher with the lower income brackets. There is a tendency for the Engel's ratio to decrease with the increase in total expenditure in both rural and urban areas.

The consumption patterns of North-Eastern Region have undergone a considerable change during the period 1994-95 to 2005-06 in which the share of food in total consumer expenditure decreases continuously. While per capita total expenditure at constant price increases gradually, the rural-urban difference increases every year. At the same time, the data of our sample survey revealed that the estimated 53 per cent of rural population in Mizoram are with MPCE of less than Rs. 840 and 35 per cent of urban population is with MPCE less than Rs. 1880. Therefore, the present analysis of expenditure pattern in the NER not only revealed the widening of the disparity between rural and urban areas, but also the existence of inequality of income and consumption among the people living in rural and urban areas. All of these undesirable trends called for public policy measures to ensure the inclusive development which include every family living in rural and urban areas.

## NOTES

1. Prasad, A.R. (2001): *Consumption Behaviour in India: Theory and Evidence.* Reliance Publishing House, New Delhi, pp. 342-343.

2. Stigler, George J. (1954): The Early History of Empirical Studies of Consumer Behaviour. *The Journal of Political Economy*, Vol. LXII, April, pp. 95-113.
3. Theil, Henri, *et al.* (1989): *International Evidence on Consumption Patterns.* Greenwich, CT JAI Press Inc.,.
   Cranfield, John A.L., *et al.* (1998): Changes in the Structure of Global Food Demand. *American Journal of Agricultural Economics*, Vol. 80, No. 5, pp. 1042-1050.
   Regmi, Anita., *et al.* (2001): Cross-Country Analysis of Food Consumption Patterns. In the *Changing Structure of Global Food Consumption and Trade.* Diane Publishing Co., Darby.
4. Bhattacharya, N. and G.S. Chatterjee (1971): On rural-urban differentials in consumer prices and per capita household consumption in India, by levels of living. *Sankhya*, Series B, Vol. 33, pp. 355-370.
5. Bhattacharya, S.S. and A.B. Roychoudhury (1980): *Regional Price Indices based on NSS 25th Round Consumer Expenditure data.* Sarvekshana, Vol. 3, No. 4, pp. 107-21.
6. NSS 60th Round (2004): *Household Consumer Expenditure in India.* Report No. 505, pp. 13.
7. As per the observation made by Economic Research Service/ USDA (1997) in its '*Cross-Country Analysis of Food Consumption Pattern'.* Working Paper No. 01-1.
8. Coondoo, Dipankor (1975): A comparison of consumer expenditure pattern of Indian middle class and working class families. *Sankhya*: *The Indian Journal of Statistics*, Vol. 37, Series C, Pt. 2, pp. 81-101.
9. Singh, Amarjit and Haramol Singh (1971): Changing Consumption Pattern In Punjab: Projections of Consumer Demand for 1973-74. *Economic and Political Weekly*, Vol. VI, No. 50.

# 4
# Estimates of Expenditure Elasticities in Mizoram

The study of consumption behaviour is basically based on the estimation and analysis of Engel's functions and the corresponding expenditure elasticities for groups of items using cross-section or time series data. In India, most of the empirical studies (Bhattacharya, 1973)[1]; Gupta, 1973[2]; Iyengar, 1967[3]; Iyenyan & Bhattacharya, 1978[4]; Coondoo, *et al.*, 1981[5]; Mazumdar, 1983[6]; Ghosh & Bhattacharya, 1995[7]) relating to consumption behaviour have concentrated on the estimation of expenditure elasticities for different item groups using cross-sectional data; though some studies (Prasad, 2001[8]; Upender, 1998[9]) used time series data. The results of these studies enable us to examine the responsiveness of consumption expenditure on particular item group to the changes in the household's total expenditures.

The expenditure elasticities for different items of consumption are very significant in economic analysis. These elasticities may be used for classifying consumer goods as 'inferior', 'necessary' and 'luxury' goods; for projecting future demand of different commodities; and for studying the impact of changes in the structure of the economy on the level of living of the people. It is, therefore, essential to obtain a precise estimate of expenditure elasticities.

The purpose of the present chapter is to estimate and analyze the Engel's function and expenditure elasticities for different commodity groups in Mizoram. An attempt is also made to analyze the changes in expenditure elasticities for various monthly per capita consumer expenditure (MPCE) classes. The whole analysis is based on the data obtained from our sample survey during July-August, 2007. The survey covered 372 households, 179 rural households and 193 urban households, in Mizoram.

## 4.1 FORMS OF ENGEL FUNCTION

The problem of finding the most appropriate form of Engel function is an old one in econometrics, but as yet no solution appears to have found general acceptance (Leser, 1963)[10]. Since the calculated expenditure elasticities depend on the type of function that has been fitted (Prais, 1953)[11], the choice of a mathematical form for the relation between expenditure on particular commodity groups and total consumer expenditure is a matter of great concern. Several studies in the past in this area suggested applying personal consideration for selecting the suitable form of the Engel function but on some grounds like the test of goodness of fit, computational simplicity etc.

In the present study, the expenditure elasticities for different commodity groups are estimated by fitting Linear and Double-Log Engel function using the method of Ordinary Least Squares (OLS). Per capita expenditures on individual groups are used as dependent variable (y) and the per capita total consumer expenditure on all the commodities as an independent variable (x). Usually per capita total consumer expenditure is used as the regressor in Engel Curve analysis. Even on the theoretical level there are strong arguments for using this variable rather than current income (Prais & Houthakher, 1955)[12]. The following functional forms are used in the present exercise:

### (a) Linear function

$$Y = b_0 + b_1X \qquad \dots (4.1)$$

The OLS estimators are

$$b_1 = \frac{n\sum XY - \sum X \sum Y}{n\sum X^2 - \left(\sum X\right)^2} \text{ and } b_0 = \overline{Y} - b_1\overline{X}$$

and the expenditure elasticity ($\eta$) is $b_1 \dfrac{\overline{X}}{\overline{Y}}$

(The elasticities are worked out at the mean values of the variables)

### (b) Double-Log function

$$Y = \alpha X^{\beta}$$

or $$\log Y = \log\alpha + \beta \log X$$

or $$\log Y = b_0 + b_1 \log X \qquad \dots (4.2)$$

Where $b_0 = \log\alpha$ and $b_1 = \beta$

The OLS estimators are

$$b_1 = \frac{n\sum(\log X)(\log Y) - \sum \log X \sum \log Y}{n\sum(\log X)^2 - \left(\sum \log X\right)^2} \quad \text{and } b_0 = \overline{\log Y} - b_1 \overline{\log X}$$

and the expenditure elasticity (η) is $b_1$

Linear function (eq. 4.1) is a simple version of Engel curve as regards to computation and interpretation of the parameters. It fulfills the condition of adding-up and homogeneity. It has its past uses in the studies by Allen & Bowley (1935)[13], Allen (1942)[14], Stone (1954)[15], Leser (1941)[16], Bhattacharya (1973)[17], Prasad (2001)[18]. Double-log function (eq. 4.2) assumes the constancy of the expenditure elasticity ($b_1$). It is independent of measurement unit, hence, can easily be applied to such Engel function as having exogenous and endogenous variables in heterogeneous units of measurement. It finds its place in the studies of Stuvel & James (1950)[19], Houthakker (1957)[20], Liviatan (1964)[21], Theil (1965)[22].

## 4.2 EMPIRICAL RESULTS

The estimated regression coefficients (i.e. $b_0$ or $\alpha$ and $b_1$ or $\beta$) and the estimated expenditure elasticities in each of the Linear and Double-log Engel function for all commodity groups under the study have been presented in Table 4.1. Except in case of clothing and housing, in which the fit of Linear function is better than Double-log function, Double-log Engel function gives a better fit than Linear Engel function in all other commodity groups. As per the statistical criteria, the functional form that has better fit would be chosen as the basis for the analysis.

The expenditure elasticity for food items is 0.44 with the coefficient of determination ($R^2$) of 0.72. Less than unity expenditure elasticity for food items indicates that the proportion spent on food items is found to decline as expenditure increases. Thus, the magnitude of expenditure elasticity on food items indicates that food can be categorized as 'necessity' in economic sense. Further, it is in conformity with the well-known Engel's Law which states that the proportion spent on food decline as income increases. Besides this, the autonomous consumption (intercept) is found to be positive. This indicates the dis-savings of the people who are in the lower income groups to maintain the minimum requirements of life.

Within the food items, the group of 'cereals, salt, sugar and edible oils' showed the lowest expenditure elasticity followed by vegetables. It is 0.14 with $R^2$ of 0.20 for 'cereals, salt, sugar and edible oils' and 0.46

**Table 4.1**: Estimated Regression Lines and Expenditure Elasticities ($\eta$) and Associated Coefficient of Determination ($R^2$) by Linear and Double-Log Engel Curves

| *Items* | *Linear Engel Function* | | | | *Double-Log Engel Function* | | | |
|---|---|---|---|---|---|---|---|---|
| | $Y = b_0 + b_1X$ | | | | $Y = \alpha X^{\beta}$ | | | |
| | $b_0$ | $b_1$ | $\eta$ | $R^2$ | $\alpha$ | $\beta$ | $\eta$ | $R^2$ |
| (1) | (2) | (3) | (4) | (5) | (6) | (7) | (8) | (9) |
| Beverages | 35.85<br>(6.6) | .053<br>(.003) | 0.74 | 0.53 | .82<br>(.24) | .69<br>(.037) | 0.69 | 0.57 |
| Meat | 57.61<br>(5.44 | .033<br>(.002) | 0.53 | 0.39 | 2.57<br>(.69) | .52<br>(.034) | 0.52 | 0.46 |
| Vegetables | 74.44<br>(5.67) | .031<br>(.002) | 0.45 | 0.34 | 4.5<br>(1.16) | 0.46 | 0.46 | 0.40 |
| Cereals, salt, sugar and edible oils | 159.33<br>(3.7) | .009<br>(.001) | 0.1 | 0.10 | 64.12<br>(7.3) | 0.14 | 0.14 | 0.20 |
| **Food Item** | **327.22**<br>**(13.7)** | **.127**<br>**(.005)** | **0.43** | **0.60** | **21.78**<br>**(2.76)** | **0.44**<br>**(.02)** | **0.44** | **0.72** |
| Pan, tobacco and intoxicants | 64.33<br>(6.15) | .03<br>(.002) | 0.47 | 0.28 | 3.53<br>(1.14) | .48<br>(.04) | 0.48 | 0.30 |
| Entertainment and telecommunications | –2.2*<br>(5.8) | .089<br>(.002) | 1.01 | 0.80 | .15<br>(.04) | .94<br>(.03) | 0.94 | 0.81 |
| Health care | 14.58<br>(6.99) | .03<br>(.003) | 0.8 | 0.24 | .27<br>(.17) | .75<br>(.08) | 0.75 | 0.25 |

**Table 4.1 (*Contd.*)**

| (1) | (2) | (3) | (4) | (5) | (6) | (7) | (8) | (9) |
|---|---|---|---|---|---|---|---|---|
| Clothing and Housing | –145.24<br>(18.2) | .284<br>(.007) | 1.4 | 0.81 | .04<br>(.01) | 1.2<br>(.04) | 1.2 | 0.79 |
| Education | – 65.09<br>(13.4) | .136<br>(.005) | 1.3 | 0.64 | .009<br>(.005) | 1.3<br>(.06) | 1.3 | 0.64 |
| Transportations | – 40.52<br>(6.4) | .055<br>(.003) | 1.6 | 0.56 | .000008<br>(.000006) | 2.02<br>(.09) | 2.02 | 0.66 |
| Miscellaneous items | –153.09<br>(21.99) | .248<br>(.009) | 1.4 | 0.68 | .001<br>(.0005) | 1.6<br>(.06) | 1.6 | 0.74 |
| **Non-food Item** | **–327.22**<br>**(13.69)** | **.873**<br>**(.005)** | **1.2** | **0.99** | **.11**<br>**(.006)** | **1.2**<br>**(.007)** | **1.2** | **0.99** |

Figures in parentheses indicate standard error estimates.

*Insignificant at 5% level of significance.

with $R^2$ of 0.40 for vegetables. These groups can be considered as the most inelastic with respect to total expenditure and income. Hence, it can be concluded that the commodity groups of 'cereals, salt, sugar and edible oils' forms the most important staple food items of the households in Mizoram. Further, the intercept term for this group is found to be positive indicating that even a slight increase in the prices of this group would result in the indebtedness of the people whose incomes are very low.

The items of beverages and meat show relatively higher expenditure elasticities (more than 0.50) among the food items considered in the study. Though this group will be considered technically as necessities, yet these groups can be considered as relatively elastic among the food items. Therefore, the sample data reveals that poor families in the State are fewer consumers of meat items. Similarly, the quantities and qualities of drinking items are, to some extent, determined by the households' income. In other words, drinking habits in Mizoram depends on the level of income.

The expenditure elasticity of non-food items is 1.2 with $R^2$ of 0.99. More than unity expenditure elasticity indicates that non-food items can be, technically, categorized as 'luxury' indicating that the proportion spent on non-food items increases with the increase in the level of total income or expenditure. It would be argued that the tastes, habits and preferences of the households change towards non-food items with the increase in income of the consumer. With the exception of pan, tobacco and intoxicants and health care, all other non-food items have more than unity elasticities.

Within non-food group, the item groups of 'pan, tobacco and intoxicants' has the lowest elasticity followed by health care. It is 0.48 with $R^2$ of 0.30 for 'pan, tobacco and intoxicants' and 0.75 with $R^2$ of 0.25 for health care. As 'pan, tobacco and intoxicants', by nature, can be addicted; its consumption would be more or less the same at all levels of incomes once an individual is addicted to it. Further, as health care is the basic necessity of life, per capita expenditure on health care would not change with the levels of incomes. Therefore, these two commodity groups would be considered 'necessity' items in Mizoram.

In case of clothing and housing, the linear Engel function gives the best estimate since $R^2$ is 0.81. The expenditure elasticity for this group is 1.4 indicating that the proportion spent on it increases with the increase in total expenditure of the consumer. More than unity elasticity implies that clothing and housing can be categorized as 'luxury' items. It implies that certain sections of the society do not afford to have such commodities.

Since 'clothing and housing' is considered as an essential commodity to man next to food, the expenditure elasticity is supposed to be less than unity. In other words, this commodity group should have been within the reach of every household. Most of the studies at a point of time, however, arrived at the conclusion that this item group fell in the class of luxury. It may be argued that the decision of incurring expenditure on this item might have been influenced by the consumption habit of neighbours reflecting demonstration effect[23].

The expenditure elasticity for education is 1.3 with $R^2$ of 0.64 and hence, the proportion spent on education increase as income increases. Technically, education can be considered as 'luxury' items. This item has become more expensive and is beyond the reach of the majority of households whose per capita income has been very low. The education, which plays a key role in human resources development, is supposed to be within the reach of the majority of population. But the numerical value of the present exercise shows that the parents who naturally look after the betterment of the children are not hesitating to incur huge amount of expenditure on education. One of the main reasons for the increasing proportion of total expenditure on education has been attributable to the emergence of private educational institutions (including professional institutions) in and outside the State.

The elasticity for transportations is 2.02 with $R^2$ of 0.66 indicating that the proportion spent on transportation increases with the increase in the level of income. Hence, transportation may be considered as 'luxury' (or ultra-luxury as its elasticity is quite high). Increased expenditure on transportations would have been the consequences of economic development along with globalization. So, it would be argued that the people with high income are more interested in travelling. Similarly, the expenditure elasticity for miscellaneous items is 1.6 with $R^2$ of 0.74. Miscellaneous items can be considered as luxury in economic sense. As a result of economic development, more items are produced in the economy and which are made available to the consumer. Hence it can be concluded that with the increase in income, the number of items consumed also increases. Therefore, the share of miscellaneous items is likely to increase with economic development.

The magnitudes of expenditure elasticities for 'entertainment and telecommunications' are 1.01 and 0.94 for linear and double-log Engel functions respectively. It indicates that the expenditure elasticity is around one. The proportion spent on this item group will remain more or less constant at all levels of incomes. Thus, this group of items may be considered as 'semi-luxury' item. It is expected that expenditure on this item group would increase as income increases. More and more facilities for this commodity group have been available to the people in recent years, to become a mass consumption good within the reach of the average person. However, it may also be argued that these facilities may not be within the reach of many rural households, while it has become essential items of consumption for the majority of the urban households. Hence, we cannot say this item as luxury or necessity and thus we call it semi-luxury items.

## 4.3 ESTIMATES OF PROPENSITIES TO CONSUME AND EXPENDITURE ELASTICITIES FOR VARIOUS MPCE CLASSES

At a given point of time, an analysis of the expenditure elasticities and propensities to consume for all commodity groups in each of the MPCE class would give a broad picture of the consumption behaviour of various sections of the society. The estimated marginal propensities and expenditure elasticities for all commodity groups in each of the MPCE class have been computed and presented in Table 4.2. Unfortunately, the estimates for most of the commodity groups are not significant for the higher MPCE classes. The estimates are more or less same for Linear and Double-Log Engel function and hence, for the sake of simplicity, the estimates by Linear Engel function will be considered for the analysis.

It is observed that the food expenditure behaves as the declining function of total expenditure over all MPCE classes. The declining marginal propensities, from 0.476 in the bottom class to 0.07 in the top MPCE class, indicate a shift in expenditure from food to non-food items with the increase income. This is in conformity with the Engel's law, the proportion of expenditure on food item decreased with the increase in the level of total expenditure.

This structural shift in the consumption pattern from food items to non-food items is positively correlated with the rise in the propensities for non-food items. The marginal propensities for non-food items increased from 0.54 in the bottom MPCE class to 0.93 in the top MPCE class. Besides this, as the expenditure elasticity for nonfood items is more than unity at all MPCE classes, non-food items can be considered as luxury items for all sections of the society. Further, the expenditure elasticity on food items is less than one in each of the PMCE class (0.83 in the bottom class to 0.45 in the top MPCE class).

**Table 4.2:** Estimates of marginal propensity to consume ($b_1$) and Expenditure Elasticities (η) for all Monthly Per Capita Consumption Expenditure (MPCE) Classes by Linear Engel's Curve (Based on the Sample Survey, July-August, 2007)

| *Items of consumption* | | *Monthly Per Capita Consumption Expenditure (Rs) Classes* | | | | | | |
|---|---|---|---|---|---|---|---|---|
| | | *0-840* | *840-1680* | *1680-2520* | *2520-3360* | *3360-4200* | *4200-+* | *All Classes* |
| Beverages | $b_1$ | 0.0497 | 0.138 | .07* | .045* | .169* | .014* | 0.053 |
| | $\eta$ | .90 | 1.6 | .72* | .58* | 2.2* | .23* | .74 |
| Meat | $b_1$ | 0.147 | 0.082 | 0.066 | .022* | –0.08* | 0.036 | 0.033 |
| | $\eta$ | 1.8 | .91 | .84* | .37* | –1.4* | 1.1* | .53 |
| Vegetables | $b_1$ | 0.188 | .038* | .034* | .018* | –0.07* | .017* | 0.031 |
| | $\eta$ | 1.3 | .43* | .44* | .28* | –1.2* | .49* | .45 |
| Cereals, salt, sugar and edible oils | $b_1$ | 0.0725 | 0.062 | .048* | –0.008 | –0.034* | .0005* | 0.009 |
| | $\eta$ | .26 | .43 | .48* | –.11* | –.58* | .02* | .10 |
| **Food Item** | $b_1$ | **0.46** | **0.32** | **0.213** | 0.08* | –0.01* | **0.068** | **0.127** |
| | $\eta$ | **.83** | **.78** | **.62** | .27* | –.04* | **.45** | **.43** |
| Pan, tobacco and intoxicants | $B_1$ | 0.04* | .014* | –0.03* | .03* | .05* | .03* | 0.03 |
| | $\eta$ | .32* | .16* | –.47* | .54* | 1.1* | .75* | .47 |
| Entertainment and telecommunications | $B_1$ | 0.099 | 0.125 | .013* | 0.149 | .124* | 0.069 | 0.089 |
| | $\eta$ | 2.7 | 1.3 | .13* | 1.5 | 1.2* | .85 | 1.01 |
| Health | $b_1$ | 0.056 | 0.073 | .03* | –0.06* | .04* | .0028* | 0.03 |
| | $\eta$ | 2 | 1.6 | .61* | –1.5* | 1.3* | .09* | .80 |
| Clothing and Housing | $b_1$ | 0.11 | 0.148 | 0.42 | 0.58 | .07* | .140* | 0.284 |
| | $\eta$ | 1.6 | 1.3 | 2.2 | 2.2 | .26* | .54* | 1.4 |

**Table 4.2** (*Contd.*)

| | | | | | | | | |
|---|---|---|---|---|---|---|---|---|
| Education | $b_1$ | 0.071 | 0.102 | 0.147 | 0.246 | .023* | .098* | 0.136 |
| | $\eta$ | 1.14 | 1.4 | 1.8 | 2.4 | .22* | .67* | 1.3 |
| Transportations | $b_1$ | 0.026 | 0.038 | .025* | 0.12 | 0.136 | 0.15 | 0.055 |
| | $\eta$ | 1.1 | 1.3 | 1.2* | 4.1 | 4.7 | 2.7 | 2.02 |
| Miscellaneous | $b_1$ | 0.142 | 0.179 | 0.186 | –0.14* | .568* | 0.44 | 0.248 |
| | $\eta$ | 1.3 | 1.3 | .97* | .91* | 3.2* | 1.8 | 1.4 |
| **Non-food Item** | $b_1$ | **0.543** | **0.68** | **0.787** | **0.923** | **1.01** | **0.932** | **0.873** |
| | $\eta$ | **1.2** | **1.2** | **1.2** | **1.3** | **1.3** | **1.1** | **1.2** |

* Insignificant at 5% level of significance.

It is also observed that the expenditure elasticity of meat is more than unity (1.8) in the bottom MPCE class against the overall elasticity of 0.53. While meat is considered to belong to the class of necessity for the whole community, it is a luxury item for the people in the bottom class. This reflects the weak purchasing power of a section of the populace, for otherwise, meat should have been within the reach of every household, is outside the reach of a number of households who are in the lower consumption bar.

Similarly, in case of the item group of health care, the expenditure elasticities for the bottom two classes turn out to be greater than unity (i.e. 2 for 0-840 class and 1.6 for 840-1680 class) against the elasticity of 0.80 for the whole community. Thus, health care is technically a luxury item for the households who are in the bottom income bracket. Consequently, it may be said that many households in the community have been deprived of health care facility, which, being an essential service should have been made accessible to all.

## 4.4 TEST OF INTER-CLASS HOMOGENEITY OF CONSUMPTION BEHAVIOUR

It has been observed in the previous section that different expenditure (MPCE) classes exhibit different consumption behaviour. For example, there is a declining tendency of the food propensities with the level of total expenditure. Similarly, while meat and health care are considered as necessities for the whole class, but they can be included among the luxury items in some classes if the criterion of expenditure elasticities is applied. This calls for the use of analytical technique to test the homogeneity of consumption behaviour for various MPCE classes.

Homogeneity of consumption behaviour does not necessarily indicate the magnitude of expenditure on a particular commodity group would be same for all classes. But, homogeneity of consumption behaviour would, rather, be indicated by the magnitude of the propensities to consume. To prove the fact of this conceptualization a mathematical formulation known as the Analysis of Variance (ANOVA) is used to test the homogeneity of the regression coefficients. The technique proceeds as follows:

Suppose we have p groups of observations on x and y. The observation in the ith group may be labeled ($x_{ij}$, $y_{ij}$), for j = 1, 2…$n_i$ and i = 1, 2, …, p. We can then have p regression equations as follows:

$$yij = \alpha_i + \beta_i (x_{ij} - x_{io}) \qquad \ldots (4.3)$$

Under the assumption that $y_{ij}$ are independently and normally distributed with Var($y_{ij}$) = $\alpha^2$ for all groups, the null hypothesis will be

$H_0 : \beta_1 = \beta_2 = \ldots\ldots\ldots\ldots = \beta_p$ (i.e. p regression lines are parallel to one another)

The Least Square estimator for ith regression line will be

$$\widehat{a}_i = y_{io} \text{ and } b_i = \frac{\sum_j (x_{ij} - x_{io})(y_{ij} - y_{io})}{\sum_j (x_{ij} - x_{io})^2} = \frac{B_i}{A_i}$$

The unrestricted residual sum of squares ($s_1^2$) is

$$s_1^2 = \sum_i \sum_j (y_{ij} - y_{jo})^2 - \sum_i b_i \sum (x_{ij} - x_{io})(y_{ij} - y_{io})$$

with degrees of freedom of $\sum_i (n_i - 2) = n - 2p$.

Similarly, the restricted residual sum of squares ($s_2^2$) is

$$s_2^2 = \sum_i \sum_j (y_{ij} - y_{io})^2 - b \sum_i \sum_j (x_{ij} - x_{io})(y_{ij} - y_{io})$$

with degrees of freedom of (*n*–*p*–1). Here '*b*' is the estimated slope coefficients for all groups or combined regression coefficient.

The format of ANOVA Table will be

| *Source of Variation* | *d.f.* | *Sum of Squares* | *Mean Square Error* | *F-statistic* |
|---|---|---|---|---|
| Difference (Total-Within groups) | p-1 | $s_2^2 - s_1^2$ | MSR = ( $s_2^2 - s_1^2$ )/(p-1) | $F = \frac{MSR}{MSE}$ |
| Within groups | n-2p | $s_1^2$ | MSE = $s_1^2$ /(n-2p) | $\sim F_{a;(p-1),(n-2p)}$ |
| Total | n-p-1 | $s_2^2$ | | |

Table 4.3 presents the value of the calculated F-statistics based on the ANOVA under the null hypothesis of equal slope coefficients of the regression lines on each of the commodity groups for all MPCE classes. The basic criteria are as follows:

If the calculated F > Theoretical F, Null Hypothesis is rejected indicating the difference of the consumption behaviour is significant, i.e. each of the MPCE class has different consumption behaviour (or significant difference in MPC).

*If F < Theoretical F, Null Hypothesis is accepted indicating that the difference in the consumption behaviour is not significant, i.e. each of the MPCE class has the same consumption behaviour (insignificant difference in MPC).*

In the following table (Table 4.3) is depicted the calculated values of F-statistics whereas the theoretical F with which to compare at 5 per cent level of significance is 2.21.

It is observed that F-statistic for food items is significant indicating that difference of consumption behaviour between each of the consumption class is significant. It confirms the result obtained in the previous section that for food the propensity to consume decreases with the increase in the level of total consumer expenditure. In case of non-food items, no significant difference of consumption behaviour is observed among the various MPCE classes, as F-ratio is less than theoretical F. It would be concluded that the amount spent on non-food items may increase with the level of total expenditure; but the propensities to consume are more or less the same for all classes. Thus, it confirms the earlier result that non-food item is luxury good for all classes of the society.

Each of the MPCE class does not show different behaviour in the consumption of 'pan, tobacco and intoxicants'; health care; education; and transportations as the calculated F's are not significant for these item groups. It may be concluded that the people in Mizoram, whether rich or poor, have the same behaviour in the consumption of these commodity groups.

At the same time, significant difference in the consumption behaviour from one MPCE class to other classes is observed in case of beverages; meat; vegetables; 'cereals, salt, sugar and edible oils'; 'entertainment and telecommunications'; 'clothing and housing'; and miscellaneous items.

**Table 4.3:** Value of F-Statistic Associated with the Analysis of Variance Applied to Test the Homogeneity of Consumption Behaviour between Various MPCE Classes

| *Sl. No* | *Items* | *F-Statistic* |
|---|---|---|
| 1. | Beverages | 5.1 |
| 2. | Meat | 4.2 |
| 3. | Vegetables | 4.4 |
| 4. | Rice, salt, sugar and edible oils | 5.2 |
| **5.** | **Food item** | **2.3** |
| 6. | Pan, tobacco and intoxicants | 0.54* |
| 7. | Entertainments and telecommunications | 2.3 |
| 8. | Health care | 1.3* |
| 9. | Clothing and housing | 4.8 |
| 10. | Education | 0.62* |
| 11. | Transportations | 0.47 |
| 12. | Miscellaneous items | 4.9 |
| **13.** | **Non-food item** | **2*** |

Theoretical F (5, 360) at 5% level of significance is 2.21. * Insignificant.

## 4.5 EFFECT OF HOUSEHOLD SIZE ON CONSUMPTION

The effect of household/family size on consumption pattern is another area of concerns especially on the consumption food items. Houthakker (1957)[24], Iyengar, *et al.* (1968)[25], Gupta (1968)[26], etc. had examined the consumption patterns using the double-log Engel function of the form

$$\log Y = a + b \log X + \log n \qquad \ldots (4.4)$$

where Y and X are household expenditure on the particular items and total expenditure respectively, and $n$ is the household size (i.e. number of persons in the family). $b$ and $c$ represent partial elasticity of expenditure to total income/expenditure and family size respectively, and $b+c$ indicates the degree of economies of scale in household consumption. No economies/diseconomies is present in consumption if $b+c = 1$. If $b+c > 1$, there is economies of scale in consumption and if $b+c < 1$, there is diseconomies in consumption with the increase in family size.

Double-log Engel function given in eq. (4.4) has been estimated for all commodities under consideration and is presented in Table 4.4. With the introduction of family size as one of the explanatory variables it was observed that $R^2$ improved significantly for all food items, and 'pan, tobacco and intoxicants', health care, 'clothing and housing', and education. With the exception of beverages, health care and transportations, the partial elasticities with respect to family sizes are significant for all items. The elasticities of consumption with respect to family sizes are significantly positive for all groups of food items and 'pan, tobacco and intoxicants'; while it is negatively significant for all other nonfood items.

One interesting things being observed is that the partial elasticity with respect to family size and total expenditure moved in the opposite direction that partial elasticity with respect to family size is most negative for the items whose elasticity with respect to total income/expenditure is highest[27].

As it was already observed in Table 4.1, the expenditure elasticities with respect to total expenditure are less than one for all food items, and 'pan, tobacco and intoxicants' and education. So, these groups can be considered as necessity items which are inelastic to the changes in income and consumption. At the same time, the elasticities are more than one for 'entertainment and telecommunications', health care, 'clothing and housing', education, transportations, miscellaneous nonfood items and total nonfood items to be considered as luxury items whose consumption depends on the changes in income.

The elasticities with respect to family size is highest for the staple food items of the state, 'cereals, salt, sugar and edible oils', which is more than the elasticity with respect to total income or expenditure. This indicates the consumption expenditure on this group is more dependent on family size rather than total expenditure or income. In addition, the partial elasticities with respect to family sizes is positively significant for all necessity items; while it is negatively significant for all luxury items. Thus, as the partial elasticities with respect to family sizes are negative for all commodities which have elastic demand with respect to total income/expenditure, family size is inversely proportional to the consumption of luxury items.

Economies of scale is found to be operative in the consumption of the following items groups: 'entertainment and telecommunications', 'clothing and housing', miscellaneous items and total nonfood item, as the sum of *b* and *c* are greater than one, though the degrees are not large.

**Table 4.4:** Partial Elasticities for Various Commodity Groups with respect to Total Expenditure (b) and Family Size (c) in Mizoram

| *Items* | *Intercept* | *Partial Elasticities* | | $R^2$ |
|---|---|---|---|---|
| | | *Slope* | | |
| | *a* | *b* | *c* | |
| Beverages | –3.2<br>(.3) | 1.1<br>(.034) | .03*<br>(.07) | .75 |
| Meat | 1.4<br>(.27) | .48<br>(.03) | .44<br>(.06) | .54 |
| Vegetables | 1.1<br>(.33) | .56<br>(.04) | .15<br>(.08) | .43 |
| Cereals, salt, sugar and edible oils | 4.1<br>(.14) | .16<br>(.02) | .81<br>(.04) | .70 |
| **Food Item** | **2.4**<br>**(.12)** | **.54**<br>**(.014)** | **.40**<br>**(.03)** | **.85** |
| Pan, tobacco and intoxicants | 1.1<br>(.4) | .51<br>(.04) | .42<br>(.09) | .37 |
| Entertainment and telecommunications | –7.6<br>(.42) | 1.7<br>(.05) | –.60<br>(.1) | .77 |
| Health care | –4.1<br>(.47) | 1.1<br>(.05) | –.23*<br>(.12) | .54 |
| Clothing and Housing | –7.2<br>(.3) | 1.7<br>(.03) | –.64<br>(.08) | .87 |
| Education | –4.6<br>(.4) | 1.3<br>(.05) | –.31<br>(.11) | .70 |
| Transportations | –4<br>(.5) | 1.04<br>(.06) | –.02*<br>(.12) | .52 |
| Miscellaneous items | –5<br>(.4) | 1.4<br>(.04) | –.23<br>(.097) | .73 |
| **Non-food Item** | **–2.8**<br>**(.08)** | **1.3**<br>**(.01)** | **–.23**<br>**(.02)** | **.98** |

*insignificant at 5% level of significance. Figures in the parenthesis indicates the standard errors of the estimates.

However, economies of scale is not clear in case of education. At the same time, diseconomies is found to be operative in the consumption of meat, vegetables, 'cereals, salt, sugar and edible oils', food item, and 'pan, tobacco and intoxicants'.

## Concluding Remarks

The expenditure elasticities of demand with respect to total expenditure or income obtained from linear and double-log Engel function revealed that the commodity group of 'cereals, salt, sugar and edible oils' formed the most important staple food items in the State of Mizoram. Since its intercept term of the function is positive, the estimated function indicates the dis-savings of the people who are at the lower income bracket to maintain the minimum food requirements. This result called for the governmental intervention to regulate the prices and supply of the food items in the state to enable the poor to get the minimum food requirements.

Education, the key for human resource development, turned out to be luxury items of consumption in the State. Certain sections of the population, particularly rural population, have financial problems to send their children to good educational institutions which are usually established in urban areas. So, the government has to device better and efficient education policy to focus on the increasing gap of educational facilities between rural and urban areas of the state. The distressing picture of the consumption behaviour in the State is the mass consumption of 'pan, tobacco and intoxicant', which has inelastic demand in all classes; the items included in the category are all injurious to health. Finally, present analysis revealed the presence of economies of scale in household consumption for all luxury items; while diseconomies have been observed in case of all necessity items.

## NOTES

1. Bhattacharya, N. (1973): *The Average Elasticity of Variable Elasticity Engel Curve.* Technical Report No. Eco/2/73, Indian Statistical Institute, Calcutta.
2. Gupta, D.B. (1973): *Consumption Pattern in India.* Tata Mc Graw Hill Publishing Co. Ltd., New Delhi.
3. Iyengar, N.S. (1967): Some Estimates of Engel Elasticities based on National Sample Survey Data. *Journal of the Royal Statistical Society*, Part I, Series A, Vol. 130.
4. Iyengar, N.S. and Bhattacharya N. (1978): *Studies on Consumer Behaviour in India.* Survey of Research in Economics, Econometrics, Vol. III. Allied Publishers, New Delhi, pp. 176-232
5. Dipankor Coondoo, Robin Mukherjee and Prasad Rao, D.S. (1981): Engel Curve Analysis with Non-monetized Consumption. *Journal of Income and Wealth*, Vol. 5, No. 2, July.

6. Mazumdar, Amita (1983): *Consumer Expenditure Pattern in India.* Technical Report No. ERU/17/83, Indian Statistical Institute, Calcutta.
7. Bhattacharya, N. (1973): *The average Elasticity of Variable Elasticity Engel Curve.* Technical Report No. Eco/2/73, Indian Statistical Institute, Calcutta.
8. Prasad, A.R. (2001): *Consumption Behaviour in India-theory and evidence.* Reliance Publishing House, New Delhi.
9. Upender, M. (1998): *Estimates of Expenditure Elasticities of Demand.* Finance India, Vol. XII, No. 3, (Sept.)
10. Leser, C.E.V. (1963): Forms of Engel Functions. *Econometrica*, Vol. 31, No. 4 (October), pp. 694-703.
11. Prais, S.J. (1953): Non-Linear Estimates of the Engel Curves. *Review of Economic Studies*, Vol. 20, pp. 87-103.
12. Prais, S.J. and H.S. Houthakker (1955): *The Analysis of Family Budgets.* Cambridge University Press.
13. Allen, R.G.D. and A.L. Bowley (1935): *Family Expenditure.* London Staples.
14. Allen, R.G.D. (1942): *Expenditure Patterns of Families of Different Types.* Studies in Mathematical Economics and Econometrics. Edited by O. Lange, F. Mc Inlyre and Th. Yutema. Chicago University Press, Chicago, Illinois.
15. Stone, R. (1954): Linear Expenditure Systems and Demand Analysis: An Application to the Pattern of British Demand. *Economic Journal*, Vol. 54, pp. 511-527.
16. Leser, C.E.V. (1941): Family Budget Data and Price-Elasticities of Demand. *The Review of Economic Studies*, Vol. 9, No. 1 (Nov.) pp. 40-57.
17. *Op. cit.*, 1.
18. *Op. cit.*, 8.
19. Stuvel, G. and S.F. James (1950): Household Expenditure on Food in Holland. Journal of the Royal Statistical Society, Series A, Vol. 113, pp. 59-80.
20. Houthakker, H.S. (1957): An International Comparison of Household Expenditure Patterns, Commemorating the Centenary of Engel's Law. *Econometrica*, Vol. 25, No. 4 (Oct.,), pp. 532-551.
21. Liviatan, N. (1964): *Consumption Pattern of Israel, Jerusalem.* Academic Press Ltd, Jerusalem.

22. Theil, H. (1965): *The Information Approach to Demand Analysis.* Econometrica, Vol. 33, No. 1, pp. 67-87.
23. Household spending may not be based on their own taste but on the tastes and expenditure of their neighbours. This idea had been put forward by Duessenbury (1949).
24. *Op. cit.,* 20.
25. Iyengar, N.S., L.R. Jain and T.N. (1968). Srinivasan: Economies of Scale in Household Consumption: *A Case Study. Indian Economic Journal,* 15, Econometric Annual, pp. 465-477.
26. Gupta, D.B. (1968): A Comparison of Consumption Patterns in Uttar Pradesh and Madras—A study of inter-regional variations with reference to India. *Indian Economic Review,* New Series, 3, pp. 129-144.
27. This is in line with the observation of H.S. Houthakker (1957) (*op. cit.*, 20)

# 5
# Comparative Analysis of Rural and Urban Consumption Behaviour

Comparative analysis of consumption behaviour between rural and urban areas would give a broad picture of the difference in the living standard of the people in the State. According to 2001 census, more than half (51%) of the population in Mizoram lived in rural areas whose main occupation is agriculture and allied activities. At the same time, the majority of urban households depend on secondary and service sectors. Differences in occupational structure lead to the difference in the attitude towards a consumption of various commodity groups. Further, there is wide disparity of facilities available for households in the two areas. A study by Sinha (1966)[1] observed a wide disparity of food consumption patterns between rural and urban areas in India. So, it is felt necessary to study the consumption pattern of rural and urban areas of Mizoram to assess the level of living of the people; even though the effects of area on consumption pattern cannot be easily identified (Prais & Houthakker, 1955)[2]. In other words, the location of human dwelling is not supposed to have much influence on consumption habits.

The present exercise tries to estimate a few parameters and to analyze the consumption patterns of rural and urban areas of Mizoram. Side by side with the analysis of consumption behaviour between the two areas, an attempt is also made to test the difference of consumption behaviour using the technique of Analysis of Covariance (ANOCOVA). An attempt is also made to analyze the consumption function in Mizoram. The whole analysis is based on the data of our Sample Survey conducted during July-August, 2007 covering 193 urban households and 179 rural households of Mizoram.

## 5.1 METHODS OF ANALYSIS

In line with the analysis in the previous Chapter, the present exercise is based on the estimation and analysis of expenditure elasticities for Linear and Double-Log Engel's functions using Ordinary Least Squares (OLS) method. The two forms of Engel's function have been fitted and the function, which has the best fit, is considered for the analysis. Per capita expenditure on individual commodity groups are used as dependent variable (Y) and the per capita total consumer expenditure on all commodities as an independent variable (X).

The following forms of Engel's functions are used in the present exercise:

### (a) Linear Function

$$Y = b_0 + b_1 X \qquad \ldots (5.1)$$

with the estimated average expenditure elasticity ($\eta$) of $b_1 \frac{\overline{X}}{\overline{Y}}$

### (b) Double-Log Function

$$Y = \alpha X\beta$$

or $$\log Y = \log\alpha + \log X$$

or $$\log Y = b_0 + b_1 \log X \qquad \ldots (5.2)$$

where $b_1$ is the constant expenditure elasticity ($\eta$).

## 5.2 EMPIRICAL RESULTS

The estimated regression lines and expenditure elasticities for linear and double-log Engel functions for various commodity groups are presented in Table 5.1 and Table 5.2. The fits of either function are better in rural areas than in urban areas for all food items. It is observed that the expenditure elasticity for food item is less than unity in rural and urban areas. Hence, the proportion of expenditure on food items decreased with the increase in total consumer expenditure. Thus, food item can be, technically, considered as 'necessity' in all areas of Mizoram.

Within food category, it is observed that the elasticity for beverages is the highest for both areas (i.e. 0.98 in rural and 0.51 in urban areas) indicating that it is the most elastic items within food category. At the same time, the item group of 'cereals, salt, sugar and edible oils' show the lowest elasticity (though the estimates are insignificant for urban areas). So, the items group of 'cereals, salt, sugar and edible oils' forms the most important staple food of the people living in rural and urban areas of Mizoram.

**Table 5.1:** Estimated Regression Lines and the Corresponding Expenditure Elasticities on Food Items for Rural and Urban Areas of Mizoram

| *Items* | | *Rural Areas* | | | | *Urban Areas* | | | |
|---|---|---|---|---|---|---|---|---|---|
| | | *Intercept* | *Slope* | *Expenditure Elasticity* | $R^2$ | *Intercept* | *Slope* | *Expenditure Elasticity* | $R^2$ |
| Beverages | a | 1.2*<br>(6.1) | 0.064<br>(.004) | **0.98** | 0.58 | 100.68<br>(12.36) | 0.037<br>(.004) | **0.478** | 0.33 |
| | B | 0.13<br>(.06) | 0.91<br>(.06) | **0.91** | 0.58 | 3.9<br>(1.6) | 0.51<br>(.052) | **0.51** | 0.38 |
| Meat | a | 27.8<br>(6.4) | 0.041<br>(.004) | **0.63** | 0.34 | 116.25<br>(8.96) | 0.0188<br>(.003) | **0.31** | 0.19 |
| | b | 0.95<br>(.5) | 0.63<br>(.06) | **0.63** | 0.38 | 13.5<br>(4.9) | 0.32<br>(.04) | **0.32** | 0.27 |
| Vegetables | a | 58.99<br>(7.6) | 0.043<br>(.006) | **0.46** | 0.29 | 89.6<br>(9.9) | 0.026<br>(.003) | **0.44** | 0.33 |
| | b | 3.6<br>(1.4) | 0.49<br>(.05) | **0.49** | 0.33 | 4.6<br>(1.9) | 0.46<br>(.052) | **0.46** | 0.33 |
| Cereals, salt, sugar and edible oil | a | 139.6<br>(4.1) | 0.016<br>(.003) | **0.09** | 0.15 | 195.76<br>(6.5) | .0004*<br>(.002) | **0.006** | 0 |
| | b | 59.6<br>(9.07) | 0.14<br>(.02) | **0.14** | 0.20 | 126.9<br>(27.6) | 0.06<br>(.03) | **0.06** | 0.02 |

**Table 5.1 (*Contd.*)**

| *Items* | | *Rural Areas* | | | | *Urban Areas* | | | |
|---|---|---|---|---|---|---|---|---|---|
| | | *Intercept* | *Slope* | *Expenditure Elasticity* | $R^2$ | *Intercept* | *Slope* | *Expenditure Elasticity* | $R^2$ |
| **Food item** | a | 227.55 | 0.163 | 0.45 | 0.70 | 502.3 | 0.083 | 0.31 | 0.38 |
| | | (11.9) | (.008) | | | (24.4) | (.008) | | |
| | b | 13.95 | 0.49 | 0.49 | 0.78 | –53.7 | 0.33 | 0.33 | 0.50 |
| | | (2.05) | (.02) | | | (11.4) | (.03) | | |

a = linear i.e. $Y = b_0 + b_1 X$, b = double-log i.e. $Y = . \alpha X^{\beta}$ and *insignificant estimate.

Figures in parentheses indicate the standard error of the respective estimate.

With the exception of vegetables, which have more or less equal elasticities for both areas, the expenditure elasticities for all other food items turn out to be significantly higher in rural areas than in urban areas. It would not be possible to draw a general conclusion temporally since at a certain range of family income the demand for food is income inelastic. However, the outcome of this analysis shows that the rural households are more responsive to the changes in total consumer expenditure or income in the consumption of food items than urban households. This is also pointing to the fact that the income earned by rural households is at a rather low range.

Table 5.2 presents the estimated regression lines and the corresponding elasticities for non-food items separately for both rural and urban areas. The expenditure elasticities of non-food items are greater than unity (i.e. 1.3 for rural and 1.2 for urban areas) indicating that the proportion spent on it increases with an increase in the total consumer expenditure. Non-food item can be considered as luxury for both rural and urban areas. In line with the earlier result of less than unit elasticity of food items, this study confirms that there is a structural shift in the consumption pattern from food to non-food items with the increase in income of the consumer. The same result is observed for both rural and urban areas.

It is interesting to note that the elasticity of only the item group of 'pan, tobacco and intoxicants' is less than unity for both areas (0.44 with $R^2$ of 0.28 in rural areas and 0.56 with $R^2$ of 0.26 in urban areas) within non-food category. The proportion spent on this group would decrease with an increase in total expenditure despite the difference in the level of income. Hence, this group can be considered as necessity for both rural and urban areas of Mizoram. There can be no denying the fact that the uses of these items are very common among the Mizo community in spite of their injurious effect to health. Furthermore, it is observed that the consumption of this items group is more responsive to changes in income of the urban households than rural households as the magnitude of the elasticity is higher in urban areas than in rural areas.

There is a significant difference of consumption behaviour between rural and urban areas for the item group of 'entertainment and telecommunications' and health care. The elasticity of 'entertainments and telecommunications' turns out to be greater than unity (i.e. 1.4) for rural areas, while it is less than unity (i.e. 0.84) for urban areas. Thus, 'entertainment and telecommunications' is luxury item for rural population while it is necessity for urban population. In the same way, the expenditure elasticity for health care is greater than unity (i.e. 1.4) in rural areas, but

**Table 5.2:** Estimated Regression Lines and the Corresponding Expenditure Elasticities on Non-Food Items for Rural and Urban Areas

| *Items* | | *Rural Areas* | | | | *Urban Areas* | | | |
|---|---|---|---|---|---|---|---|---|---|
| | | *Intercept* | *Slope* | ***Expenditure Elasticity*** | $R^2$ | *Intercept* | *Slope* | ***Expenditure Elasticity*** | $R^2$ |
| (1) | (2) | (3) | (4) | (5) | (6) | (7) | (8) | (9) | (10) |
| Pan, tobacco and intoxicants | a | 60.5<br>(7.2) | 0.035<br>(.005) | **0.389** | 0.23 | 62.39<br>(11.79) | 0.029<br>(.004) | **0.56** | 0.24 |
| | b | 4.7<br>(1.9) | 0.44<br>(.06) | **0.44** | 0.28 | 1.72<br>(1.03) | 0.56<br>(.07) | **0.56** | 0.26 |
| Entertainment and telecommunications | a | –38.2<br>(4.98) | 0.114<br>(.003) | **1.4** | 0.87 | 37.38<br>(11.42) | 0.077<br>(.004) | **0.84** | 0.71 |
| | b | 0.01<br>(.004) | 1.3<br>(.04) | **1.3** | 0.86 | 0.35<br>(.12) | 0.83<br>(.041) | **0.83** | 0.71 |
| Health care | a | –26.6<br>(9.2) | 0.07<br>(.006) | **1.4** | 0.44 | 31.83<br>(10.94) | 0.0211<br>(.003) | **0.64** | 0.16 |
| | b | .004*<br>(.004) | 1.4<br>(.14) | **1.4** | 0.44 | 0.54<br>(0.48) | 0.65<br>(.11) | **0.65** | 0.16 |
| Clothing and housing | a | –201.2<br>(18.19) | 0.38<br>(.01) | **1.9** | 0.84 | –188.36<br>(34.07) | 0.283<br>(.01) | **1.4** | 0.78 |
| | b | 0.0009<br>(.0004) | 1.7<br>(.06) | **1.7** | 0.88 | 0.04<br>(.02) | 1.2<br>(.06) | **1.2** | 0.77 |

**Table 5.2 (*Contd.*)**

| (1) | (2) | (3) | (4) | (5) | (6) | (7) | (8) | (9) | (10) |
|---|---|---|---|---|---|---|---|---|---|
| Education | a | –41.53<br>(10.6) | 0.122<br>(.007) | **1.4** | 0.62 | –94.66<br>(28.96) | 0.145<br>(.009) | **1.32** | 0.57 |
| | b | 0.002<br>(.0017) | 1.5<br>(.097) | **1.5** | 0.65 | 0.011<br>(.009) | 1.3<br>(.09) | **1.3** | 0.57 |
| Transportations | a | –3.498*<br>(4.88) | 0.036<br>(.003) | **1.09** | 0.41 | –93.92<br>(12.98) | 0.0698<br>(.004) | **1.97** | 0.60 |
| | b | 0.04<br>(.03) | 0.99<br>(.1) | **0.99** | 0.41 | .000002*<br>(.000002) | 2.2<br>(.13) | **2.2** | 0.69 |
| Miscellaneous | a | 22.98<br>(8.9) | 0.081<br>(.006) | **0.8** | 0.51 | –256.98<br>(44.48) | 0.292<br>(.01) | **1.5** | 0.70 |
| | b | 0.51<br>(.24) | 0.79<br>(.06) | **0.79** | 0.52 | .002*<br>(.002) | 1.5<br>(.08) | **1.5** | 0.72 |
| **Non-food item** | **a** | **–227.55<br>(11.94)** | **0.837<br>(.008)** | **1.3** | **0.98** | **–502.33<br>(24.39)** | **0.917<br>(.008)** | **1.25** | **0.99** |
| | **b** | **0.09<br>(.008)** | **1.3<br>(.011)** | **1.3** | **0.99** | **0.102<br>(.008)** | **1.2<br>(.0096)** | **1.2** | **0.99** |

*a* = linear i.e. $Y = b_0 + b_1 X$, *b* = double–log i.e. Y=. $\alpha X^{\beta}$ and *insignificant estimate.

Figures in parentheses indicate the standard error of the respective estimate it is less than unity (i.e. 0.64) for urban areas. Technically, health care can be classified as luxury item for rural population; but it is necessity for urban population. So, in rural areas the attainment of healthcare depends on family income which implies a number of families are deprived of proper healthcare facilities.

Following the above observations it may be argued that the items group of 'entertainment and telecommunications' has become the basic consumption items of the majority of urban households. However, in rural areas, the services of this kind are not provided unless the effort is well worth the cost. Because this is a type of utility with a strong demonstration effect, its consumption would spread with amazing rapidity once it is within the reach of the households at large. Hence, it is found to be highly elastic among the rising income-group of rural community. Likewise, expenditure on health care activities highly depends on the income of rural households. This is a clear indication that many rural households do not have any access to health care facilities. From the viewpoint of welfare economics, the government is required to treat health-care as public goods whose provision should be made available through budgetary means. Such provisions are justified on account of market failure and the possibility of immense external benefits that should have accrued to the community.

Within non-food items, significant difference has also been observed in case of miscellaneous items. The elasticity of this item is less than unity (0.79 with $R^2$ of 0.52) in rural areas, while it is greater than unity (1.5 with $R^2$ of 0.52) in urban areas. Therefore, the miscellaneous items belongs to the class of necessity for rural population; whereas, it is luxury for urban population. The consumption of miscellaneous items is not highly dependent upon total consumer expenditure for rural population. It may be argued that many items that are consumed in urban areas are not available in rural areas. These items are, basically, supposed to be luxury items. In addition to these items, it has been found that the elasticities for other nonfood groups are more than unity for both rural and urban areas. Hence, the items groups of 'clothing and housing'; education; and transportations are luxury items for both rural and urban populations.

## 5.3 EFFECTS OF FAMILY SIZE ON HOUSEHOLDS' CONSUMPTION

We have elaborated the household consumer expenditure elasticities in both rural and urban areas of Mizoram without considering the possible effects of family size on household consumer expenditure patterns. Some studies, Houthakker (1957)[3], Iyengar, *et al.* (1968)[4], Gupta (1968)[5], in the past observed that family size played a significant effects on household consumption patterns. Partial elasticities with respect to family size are found to be positive in these studies in case of food items; while it was negative for non-food, especially for luxury items of consumption.

In an attempt to determine the effect of family size on household consumption, the following double-logarithmic engel curve has been estimated:

$$\log Y = a + b \log X + c \log n \quad \dots (5.3)$$

where Y is the expenditure on particular group of commodity, X is the total household consumer expenditure, *n* is the family size, *a* and *b* are the partial elasticities with respect to total expenditure and family size respectively. Here, *a*+*b* determines the level economies of scale in household consumption on a particular item. If it is more than 1, there is economies of scale in household consumption with an increase in family size; and if it is less than 1, there exists diseconomies of scale with an increase in family size.

The estimated partial elasticities on total expenditure (b) and family size (c) for rural and urban areas of Mizoram has been given in Table 5.3. With the introduction of family size as one of the explanatory variables, the coefficients of determination ($R^2$) improved in all food items for both rural and urban areas. However, no significant improvement of $R^2$ is being observed in case of non food items.

In rural areas, except for the case of beverages and vegetables which have insignificant partial elasticities with respect to family size, partial elasticities with respect to family size are significantly positive for the consumption of all food items and 'pan, tobacco and intoxicants'. But it is significantly negative for all other items. In urban areas, elasticities with respect to family size are significantly positive for all groups of food items, 'pan, tobacco and intoxicants' and 'clothing and housing'. In other words, family size significantly affects household consumption patterns for all food items, 'pan, tobacco and intoxicants' and 'clothing and housing'; but the elasticity is significantly negative on the consumption of the remaining items of consumption. Greater partial elasticity on family size in case of clothing and housing than total expenditure reflects the difficulty of maintaining larger families in urban areas.

**Table 5.3:** Partial Elasticities for Various Commodity Groups with respect total Expenditure (b) and Family Size (c) in Rural and Urban Areas of Mizoram

| *Items* | *Rural Areas* | | | *Urban Areas* | | |
|---|---|---|---|---|---|---|
| | *Partial Elasticities* | | $R^2$ | *Partial Elasticities* | | $R^2$ |
| | *B* | *c* | | *b* | *c* | |
| Beverages | 1.11<br>(.06) | –.18*<br>(.11) | .72 | .68<br>(.05) | .31<br>(.09) | .55 |
| Meat | .42<br>(.05) | .43<br>(.09) | .55 | .36<br>(.049) | .58<br>(.08) | .43 |
| Vegetables | .62<br>(.076) | .09*<br>(.14) | .36 | .58<br>(.05) | .16*<br>(.09) | .42 |
| Cereals, salt, sugar and edible oils | .15<br>(.025) | .82<br>(.05) | .76 | .05*<br>(.03) | .85<br>(.05) | .61 |
| **Food Item** | **.55**<br>**(.02)** | **.37**<br>**(.04)** | **.88** | **.404**<br>**(.03)** | **.51**<br>**(.05)** | **.71** |
| Pan, tobacco and intoxicants | .51<br>(.06) | .38<br>(.12) | .41 | .68<br>(.09) | .38<br>(.15) | .30 |
| Entertainment and teleco-mmunications | 2.11<br>(.09) | –1.3<br>(.16) | .78 | 1.07<br>(.05) | .098*<br>(.087) | .73 |
| Health care | 1.7<br>(.08) | –.88<br>(.14) | .74 | .48<br>(.098) | .29*<br>(.17) | .15 |
| Clothing and Housing | 1.8<br>(.06) | –.87<br>(.11) | .85 | .24*<br>(.14) | .52<br>(.24) | .05 |
| Education | 1.2<br>(.08) | –.25*<br>(.13) | .65 | 1.5<br>(.08) | –.398<br>(.15) | .65 |
| Transportations | 1.04<br>(.07) | –.02*<br>(.13) | .62 | 1.4<br>(.11) | –.25*<br>(.19) | .48 |
| Miscellaneous items | 1.2<br>(.08) | .05*<br>(.15) | .61 | 1.22<br>(.07) | –.34<br>(.12) | .62 |
| **Non-food Item** | **1.34**<br>**(.02)** | **–.28**<br>**(.04)** | **.97** | **1.27**<br>**(.013)** | **–.203**<br>**(.023)** | **.98** |

*insignificant at 5% level of significance.
Figures in parenthesis indicates the standard error.

It is interesting to note that the effect of family size is found to be significantly more than the affects of total household expenditure or income in the consumption of 'cereals, salt, sugar and edible oils' in rural and urban areas. So, it is the number of persons in the family rather than total income or expenditure that explains the consumption of this item group. As it has already been observed in the previous Chapter, the elasticity on family size is most negative for the item which has the highest elasticity on total consumer expenditure.

In rural areas, economies of scale are found to be operative in the consumption of transportations, miscellaneous and total food items; whereas, diseconomies are operative in the consumption of all other groups. At the same time, in urban areas, economies of scale is found to be operative in the consumer expenditure on transportations, education and total nonfood items; while diseconomies is found to be operative in all groups of food items, 'pan, tobacco and intoxicants', 'entertainment and telecommunications', health care, 'clothing and housing', and miscellaneous items.

## 5.4 TEST OF THE HOMOGENEITY OF RURAL-URBAN CONSUMPTION BEHAVIOUR

The differences of consumption behaviour between rural and urban areas of Mizoram have been analyzed in the previous section. It has been observed that the two areas show different behaviour in the consumption of some commodity groups. However, same behaviour has been observed for some items. Hence, it is felt necessary to precisely test the homogeneity of consumption behaviour for all commodity groups using a suitable statistical method. So we have decided to use the method of Analysis of Covariance (ANOCOVA) to test the difference in Engel curves between rural and urban areas of Mizoram. The technique of ANOCOVA was also applied to test the differences in consumption patterns in the studies by Maitra (1969)[6], Jain and Tendulkar (1973)[7], and Coondoo (1975)[8].

### 5.4.1 Description of Analysis of Covariance (ANOCOVA) Model

Let $Y_{ri}$, $X_{ri}$ ($r = 1, 2; i = 1, 2, \ldots, n$), and there are $n_1$ and $n_2$ ($n = n_1 + n_1$) observations in rural and urban areas respectively, indicate the appropriate partitioning of the data. The simple regression equation of expenditure on particular commodity (Y) on total expenditure (X) can be expressed as:

$$Y = X\beta + U$$

or

$$\begin{bmatrix} y_1 \\ y_2 \\ .. \\ y_n \end{bmatrix} = \begin{bmatrix} 1 & x_1 \\ 1 & x_2 \\ .. & .. \\ 1 & x_n \end{bmatrix} \begin{bmatrix} b_1 \\ b_2 \end{bmatrix} + \begin{bmatrix} u_1 \\ u_2 \\ .. \\ u_n \end{bmatrix} \quad \text{... (5.4)}$$

Equation (5.4) does not consider the class (area) effect in the total variation. It merely indicates the variation in Y explained by the variation in X variables. If we, however, wish to investigate the possible existence of class effect in the form of different intercepts, we would postulate a more general model by introducing the matrix of 'Dummy variables'.

$$Y = D\alpha + X\beta + U$$

or

$$\begin{bmatrix} y_{11} \\ y_{12} \\ .. \\ y_{1n_1} \\ y_{21} \\ y_{22} \\ .. \\ y_{2n_2} \end{bmatrix} = \begin{bmatrix} 0 & 1 & x_{11} \\ 0 & 1 & x_{12} \\ .. & .. & .. \\ 0 & 1 & x_{1n_1} \\ 1 & 1 & x_{21} \\ 1 & 1 & x_{22} \\ .. & .. & .. \\ 1 & 1 & x_{2n_2} \end{bmatrix} \begin{bmatrix} a \\ b_1 \\ b_2 \end{bmatrix} + \begin{bmatrix} u_1 \\ u_2 \\ .. \\ u_n \end{bmatrix}$$

*or*

$$Y = b_1 + b_2 X_i$$

$$Y = (a + b_1) + b_2 X_i \quad \text{... (5.5)}$$

If there is no class (area) effect, $\alpha = 0$. Hence, the appropriate hypothesis will be

$$H_0: \alpha = 0.$$

Applying OLS to Eq. (5.4) gives the residual sum of squares (RSS) of

$$s's = Y'Y - \hat{\beta}X'Y \quad \text{... (5.6)}$$

Likewise, if we apply OLS to Eq. (5.5), the RSS will be

$$e'e = Y'Y - \tilde{\alpha}'D'Y - \tilde{\beta}X'Y \quad \text{... (5.7)}$$

The reduction in RSS in moving from Eq. (5.4) to Eq. (5.5) is then s's – e'e.

So far, the model assumes constant slope coefficients. Now, we must allow the slope to vary from rural to urban areas as well as the intercepts. This amounts simply to running separate regression for each area. The Least Square lines for both areas may then be

$$Y_1 = X_1 b_1 + r_1$$
$$Y_2 = X_2 b_2 + r_2 \qquad \dots (5.8)$$

If we define a block-diagonal matrix Z as

$$Z = \begin{bmatrix} X_{1i} & 0 \\ 0 & X_{2i} \end{bmatrix}$$

(Note that the first column of each of the X matrix consists ones to allow a single intercept)

Then Eq. (5.7) reduces to

$$Y = Zb + r \qquad \dots (5.9)$$

Application of OLS to Eq. (5.9) gives RSS of

$$r'r = Y'Y - \hat{b}'Z'Y$$

Thus, the complete ANOCOVA model may be summarized in the following table:

**Table 5.4**

| *Source* | *Sum of Squares* | *d.f.* | *Mean Square Error* |
|---|---|---|---|
| Z | Residual: $r'r = s_4$ | n–2k | $MS_4 = s_4/(n-2k)$ |
| | Incremental (differential slopes) $e'e - r'r = s_3$ | k – 1 | $MS_3 = s_3/(k-1)$ |
| X and D | Residual: $e'e = s_2$ | n – k –1 | $MS_2 = s_2/(n-k-1)$ |
| | Incremental (differential intercepts) $s's - e'e = s_1$ | p–1=1 | $MS_1 = s_1$ |
| X | Residual: s's | n – k | |

*Note*: k is the number of parameters (i.e. 2 for the present analysis), p is number of classes (i.e. 2) and n is the total number of observations.

Thus, we can define the following test statistic:

1. Test of differential intercepts: $F_{(1)} = \dfrac{MS_1}{MS_2} \sim F_{1,(n-k-1)}$

2. Test of differential slope coefficients: $F_{(2)} = \dfrac{MS_3}{MS_4} \sim F_{(k-1),(n-2k)}$

3. Test for overall homogeneity: $F_{(3)} = \dfrac{MS_1 + MS_2}{MS_4} \sim F_{2,(n-2k)}$

The following hypotheses are being tested for the estimated Engel's curves between rural and urban areas for all commodity groups:

1. Equal intercept terms (i.e. $\alpha = 0$)
2. Equal slope coefficients.
3. Equality of overall regression estimates.

*The test criteria*:

If calculated F < theoretical F, accept the null hypothesis (i.e. no difference)

- *theoretical F, reject the null hypothesis (i.e. significant difference)*

## 5.4.2 Results of the Analysis of Covariance Test

The result of the Analysis of Covariance (ANOCOVA) is presented in Table 5.4. The analysis reveals that households in rural and urban areas of Mizoram have differing behaviour in the consumption of beverages; meat; vegetables; 'cereals, salt, sugar and edible oils'; all food items; 'entertainment and telecommunications'; health care; clothing and housing'; transportations; miscellaneous items; and all non-food items as the calculated F's for these commodity groups are greater than theoretical F at 5 per cent level of significance. In case of vegetables, the difference of intercept terms is not significant. So, vegetables have the same intercept but different slopes for rural and urban areas. It can, still, be said that the two areas have different behaviour in the consumption of vegetables because the marginal propensities (slopes) are significantly different from each other.

In case of 'pan, tobacco and intoxicants', and education, rural and urban areas do not show any significant difference of consumption behaviour. Thus, it can be concluded that the rural and urban households have the same behaviour in the consumption of these two commodity groups.

**Table 5.5:** Value of F-Ratio Associated with Different Null Hypothesis Underlying the Analysis of Covariance Applied to Test the Homogeneity of Expenditure Patterns for Different Items between Rural and Urban Areas (Based on the Sample Survey during July-August, 2007, data)

| *Sl. No* | *Items* | *F(1)* | *F(2)* | *F(3)* |
|---|---|---|---|---|
| 1. | Beverages | 43.57 | 16.24 | 23.07 |
| 2. | Meat | 56.94 | 16.57 | 30.19 |
| 3. | Vegetables | 0.44* | 7.32 | 3.88 |
| 4. | Cereals, salt, sugar and edible oils | 41.99 | 16.81 | 30.29 |
| 5. | Food Items | 70.84 | 38.27 | 58.14 |
| 6. | Pan, tobacco and intoxicants | 0.69* | 0.82* | 0.75* |
| 7. | Entertainments and telecommunications | 5.26 | 39.07 | 22.44 |
| 8. | Health Care | 4.45 | 54.35 | 29.72 |
| 9. | Clothing and housing | 273.8 | 87.63 | 125.22 |
| 10. | Education | 0.86* | 2.49* | 1.68* |
| 11. | Transportations | 18.6 | 26.57 | 23.23 |
| 12. | Miscellaneous Items | 4.91 | 100.36 | 53.3 |
| 13. | Non-Food Items | 70.84 | 38.27 | 39 |

(a) Theoretical $F_{(1, 369)}(.05)$ corresponding to $F_{(1)}$ 3.84;

(b) Theoretical $F_{(1, 368)}(.05)$ corresponding to $F_{(2)}$ is 3.84;

(c) Theoretical $F_{(2, 368)}$ (.05) corresponding to $F_{(3)}$ is 3.00;

* Insignificant at 5% level of significance.

*Note*: Details of analysis are given in Table 5.7 at the end of the chapter.

Following the above results, it may be concluded that rural and urban areas of Mizoram have shown different consumption behaviour for food and non-food items, though the same behaviour is observed in two sub-groups of non-food items.

## 5.5 ESTIMATES OF CONSUMPTION FUNCTION

There is a long tradition of theoretical and empirical works on consumption function. Keynes (1936)[9] postulated that consumption is a function of absolute income. This is known, in consumption theory, as Absolute Income Hypothesis (AIH). Keynes postulated the hypotheses that the consumption expenditure is a stable function of real income and the marginal propensity to consume is positive but less than one. However, theoretical and empirical limitations of AIH led to a number of hypotheses in the subsequent years[10]. We will not go into detail analysis of the theories of consumption function because it has been elaborated in the earlier chapter.

In the present exercise, the consumption function in respect of Mizoram as well as separate estimates of consumption functions for rural and urban Mizoram have been calculated with the method of Ordinary Least Square (OLS). The Linear and Double-log consumption function are estimated. The total per capita monthly consumer expenditure on all items is used as dependent variable (C) while per capita monthly income has been used as an independent variable (Y). The estimated consumption functions have been presented in Table 5.6.

It is observed that the fits of double-log function are better than linear function (as $R^2$ are high) in all cases. Hence, the present exercise will be, according to statistical criteria, based on the estimates of double-log function.

**Table 5.6:** Estimates of Consumption Function

| | *Functions* | $R^2$ | *MPC* | *APC* |
|---|---|---|---|---|
| Mizoram | $C = 543.46 + 0.59\ Y$ | 0.88 | 0.59 | 0.82 |
| | $\log C = 1.88 + 0.74 \log Y$ | 0.90 | 0.61 | |
| Rural | $C = 271.56 + 0.71\ Y$ | 0.81 | 0.71 | 0.93 |
| | $\log C = 1.49 + 0.79 \log Y$ | 0.83 | 0.74 | |
| Urban | $C = 846.53 + 0.54\ Y$ | 0.87 | 0.54 | 0.78 |
| | $\log C = 2.096 + 0.72 \log Y$ | 0.87 | 0.54 | |

The estimated marginal propensity to consume (MPC) of Mizoram is 0.61 with $R^2$ of 0.90, which implies that the income elasticity of consumption is less than unity (i.e. 0.74). Less than unity elasticity further indicates that the average propensity to consume (APC) decrease with an increase in income of the consumer. From this result, it is also evident that there is a wide disparity of consumption behaviour between rural and urban areas. The MPC of rural areas (i.e. 0.74) is significantly greater than the urban MPC (i.e. 0.56). Eventually, it is possible to conclude that the consumption function in respect of rural population is more responsive to the changes in income. Further, the fits are better in urban areas than in rural areas for both types of consumption functions[11].

The autonomous consumption (intercept term) is found to be positive for both functional forms. Positive autonomous consumption indicates the dis-savings of the people who are at the bottom income range. Further, the average propensity to consume (APC) is less than marginal propensity to consume (MPC) in all cases (i.e. MPC<APC). Hence, the contention

of Absolute Income Hypothesis that MPC < APC is found to be true in our analysis.

Side by side with the marginal propensity to consume analyzed so far, it is considered necessary to elaborate what is happening in saving function. It is well known in economic theory that what is not consumed is saved and hence, the saving propensities and the corresponding income elasticity of saving have been worked out from the corresponding consumption function.

Table 5.7 presents the average propensity to save (APS) and marginal propensity to save (MPS) corresponding to the consumption function given above.

**Table 5.7:** Propensities to Saves for Rural and Urban Areas of Mizoram

| | *APS* | *MPS* | *Income Elasticity to Save* |
|---|---|---|---|
| Rural Areas | 0.07 | 0.26 | 3.7 |
| Urban Areas | 0.22 | 0.44 | 1.99 |
| Mizoram | 0.18 | 0.39 | 2.12 |

The average propensity to save (APS) is 0.07 and 0.22 for rural and urban areas respectively. At the same time, the marginal propensity to save (MPS) is 0.26 and 0.44 for rural and urban areas respectively. The overall results to a great extent revealed the diversity in saving behaviour. The rural sector appears to have an extremely low saving rate. As the MPS for urban areas is significantly higher than that of rural areas, it can be said that urban population has better saving habit than rural population. However, as the income elasticity of saving is quite high, there exist a high saving potential in rural areas with the development of the economy. Further, since the investment multiplier, which is the inverse of marginal propensity to save, is higher (i.e. 3.85) in rural areas than in urban areas (i.e. 2.27), any governmental effort to develop rural areas by increasing public expenditure would result more income through the working of multiplier in rural areas than in urban areas.

Looking at the overall picture of the State, the income elasticity of saving is greater than unity (i.e. 2.12). This indicates the average propensity to save increases as income increases and conversely, the average propensity to consume decreases as income increases. In other words, the result that has emerged from this study reveals that saving is an increasing function of income.

As it has already been observed, there is a wide disparity of consumption/saving behaviour between rural and urban areas of Mizoram. It is necessary to precisely test the difference in consumption behaviour using suitable method. Since the difference of intercept terms is quite high between rural and urban areas, it is considered appropriate to test only the slope (MPC) of the consumption function. A test statistic developed by Chow (1960)[12], called the Chow Test, is adopted for testing significance of the difference in consumption behaviour.

Consider the following two consumption functions for rural areas ($C_1$) and urban areas ($C_2$) respectively

$$C_1 = a_1 + b_1 Y_1 + e_1$$
$$C_2 = a_1 + b_1 Y_2 + e_2 \qquad \text{... (5.10)}$$

Where $Y_1$ and $Y_2$ are the total disposable income in rural areas and urban areas respectively, $e_1$ and $e_2$ are error/residual terms. The test statistic underlying the null hypothesis of equal slope coefficients, i.e. $H_0 : \beta_1 = \beta_2$,

$$F = \frac{\left[\sum e_p^2 - (\sum e_1^2 + \sum e_2^2)\right]/k}{(\sum e_1^2 + \sum e_2^2)/(n_1 + n_2 - 2k)} \qquad \text{...(5.11)}$$

is given by follows F-statistic with ($k$, $n_1$+$n_2$–$2k$) degrees of freedom. Where $k$ is the number of parameters (i.e. 2 in the present analysis), the subscript $p$ denotes pooled (i.e. whole area taken together), and $n_1$ and $n_2$ are the number of observations in rural and urban areas respectively. The result of Chow test is given in Table 5.8.

**Table 5.8:** The Chow Test for the Equality of Regressions between Rural and Urban Areas Under the Null Hypothesis of Equal Slope Coefficients (MPC)

| *Unexplained Variation* | | *RSS* | *df* | *MS* | *F* |
|---|---|---|---|---|---|
| Rural | RSS(1) | 29849952.29 | 177 | 168643.8 | |
| Urban | RSS (2) | 65748702.89 | 191 | 344234 | |
| Combined (Rural + Urban) | RSS(a) | 95598655.18 | 368 | 259779 | |
| Pooled (Mizoram) | RSS(p) | 108927576.7 | 370 | 294398.9 | |
| Difference | RSS(p)–RSS(a) | 13328921.51 | 2 | 6664461 | 25.65 |

Since the calculated F = 25.65 is significantly higher than theoretical F-statistic at all level of significance, the null hypothesis of equal slope coefficients (MPC) for both rural and urban areas is rejected. This test confirms the earlier results of the existence of wide disparity of consumption/saving behaviour between rural and urban areas. Hence, it can be concluded that rural and urban areas of Mizoram exhibit significantly different consumption behaviour as well as saving behaviour.

## Concluding Remarks

The analysis that have been made in this chapter revealed that rural areas of Mizoram has higher food propensity to consume than urban areas, which implies the lower standard of living and development in rural areas than urban areas. The estimated rural saving rate and saving propensity are very low comparing with urban rate. However, the investment multiplier is higher in rural areas and hence, public expenditures in the rural areas are expected to have greater impact on the standard of living in rural areas than urban areas through the working of multiplier. Present analysis proved that there is no difference in consumption behaviour between the rural and urban areas in case of 'pan, tobacco and intoxicants' and education. Therefore, it is clear that every household in Mizoram has to spend their income on education and 'pan, tobacco and intoxicants' whatever may be their income.

**Table 5.9:** Analysis of Covariance (ANOCOVA) to Test the Homogeneity of Consumption Behaviour Between Rural and Urban Areas for Various Commodity Groups

### 1. Beverages

| *Source* | *RSS* | *df* | *Mean Square* | *F(1)* | *F(2)* | *F(3)* |
|---|---|---|---|---|---|---|
| Z | 1931609.528 | 368 | 5248.938935 | 43.57 | 16.24 | 23.07 |
| | (Incremental Slope) | | | | | |
| | 85254.472 | 1 | 85254.472 | | | |
| X and D | 2016864 | 369 | 5465.756098 | | | |
| | (Incremental intercept) | | | | | |
| | 238161 | 1 | 238161 | | | |
| X | 2255025 | 370 | | | | |

## 2. Meat

| *Source* | *RSS* | *df* | *Mean Square* | *F(1)* | *F(2)* | *F(3)* |
|---|---|---|---|---|---|---|
| Z | 1288436.36 | 368 | 3501.185761 | 56.94 | 16.57 | 30.19 |
| | (Incremental Slope) | | | | | |
| | 58016.19 | 1 | 58016.19 | | | |
| X and D | 1346452.55 | 369 | 3648.9229 | | | |
| | (Incremental intercept) | | | | | |
| | 207757.45 | 1 | 207757.45 | | | |
| X | 1554210 | 370 | | | | |

## 3. Vegetables

| *Source* | *RSS* | *df* | *Mean Square* | *F(1)* | *F(2)* | *F(3)* |
|---|---|---|---|---|---|---|
| Z | 1656729.862 | 368 | 4501.983321 | 0.44 | 7.32 | 3.88 |
| | (Incremental Slope) | | | | | |
| | 32968.428 | 1 | 32968.428 | | | |
| X and D | 1689698.29 | 369 | 4579.128157 | | | |
| | (Incremental intercept) | | | | | |
| | 1993.71 | 1 | 1993.71 | | | |
| X | 1691692 | 370 | | | | |

## 4. Cereals, Salt, Sugar and Edible Oils

| *Source* | *RSS* | *df* | *Mean Square* | *F(1)* | *F(2)* | *F(3)* |
|---|---|---|---|---|---|---|
| Z | 620084.6379 | 368 | 1685.012603 | 41.99 | 16.81 | 30.29 |
| | (Incremental Slope) | | | | | |
| | 28317.0111 | 1 | 28317.0111 | | | |
| X and D | 648401.649 | 369 | 1757.186041 | | | |
| | (Incremental intercept) | | | | | |
| | 73785.651 | 1 | 73785.651 | | | |
| X | 722187.3 | 370 | | | | |

### 5. Food Item

| *Source* | *RSS* | *df* | *Mean Square* | *F(1)* | *F(2)* | *F(3)* |
|---|---|---|---|---|---|---|
| Z | 7492032.949 | 368 | 20358.78519 | 70.84 | 38.27 | 58.14 |
| | (Incremental Slope) | | | | | |
| | 779155.781 | 1 | 779155.781 | | | |
| X and D | 8271188.73 | 369 | 22415.14561 | | | |
| | (Incremental intercept) | | | | | |
| | 1587977.27 | 1 | 1587977.27 | | | |
| X | 9859166 | 370 | | | | |

### 6. Pan, Tobacco and Intoxicants

| *Source* | *RSS* | *df* | *Mean Square* | *F(1)* | *F(2)* | *F(3)* |
|---|---|---|---|---|---|---|
| Z | 1982380.14 | 368 | 5386.902554 | 0.69 | 0.82 | 0.75 |
| | (Incremental Slope) | | | | | |
| | 4405.38 | 1 | 4405.38 | | | |
| X and D | 1986785.52 | 369 | 5384.242602 | | | |
| | (Incremental intercept) | | | | | |
| | 3712.48 | 1 | 3712.48 | | | |
| X | 1990498 | 370 | | | | |

### 7. Entertainment and Telecommunications

| *Source* | *RSS* | *df* | *Mean Square* | *F(1)* | *F(2)* | *F(3)* |
|---|---|---|---|---|---|---|
| Z | 1560197.848 | 368 | 4239.668065 | 5.26 | 39.07 | 22.44 |
| | (Incremental Slope) | | | | | |
| | 165649.812 | 1 | 165649.812 | | | |
| X and D | 1725847.66 | 369 | 4677.09393 | | | |
| | (Incremental intercept) | | | | | |
| | 24597.34 | 1 | 24597.34 | | | |
| X | 1750445 | 370 | | | | |

**8. Health Care**

| *Source* | *RSS* | *df* | *Mean Square* | *F(1)* | *F(2)* | *F(3)* |
|---|---|---|---|---|---|---|
| Z | 2214477.849 | 368 | 6017.602851 | 4.45 | 54.35 | 29.72 |
| | (Incremental Slope) | | | | | |
| | 327037.65 | 1 | 327037.65 | | | |
| X and D | 2541515.5 | 369 | 6887.575881 | | | |
| | (Incremental intercept) | | | | | |
| | 30661.5 | 1 | 30661.5 | | | |
| X | 2572177 | 370 | | | | |

**9. Clothing and Housing**

| *Source* | *RSS* | *df* | *Mean Square* | *F(1)* | *F(2)* | *F(3)* |
|---|---|---|---|---|---|---|
| Z | 54118728.44 | 368 | 147061.7621 | 273.8 | 87.63 | 125.2 |
| | (Incremental Slope) | | | | | |
| | 12886821.56 | 1 | 12886821.56 | | | |
| X and D | 67005550 | 369 | 181586.8564 | | | |
| | (Incremental intercept) | | | | | |
| | –4.95E+07 | 1 | –49546170.16 | | | |
| X | 17459379.84 | 370 | | | | |

**10. Education**

| *Source* | *RSS* | *df* | *Mean Square* | *F(1)* | *F(2)* | *F(3)* |
|---|---|---|---|---|---|---|
| Z | 9441625.349 | 368 | 25656.59062 | 0.86 | 2.49 | 1.68 |
| | (Incremental Slope) | | | | | |
| | 64003.551 | 1 | 64003.551 | | | |
| X and D | 9505628.9 | 369 | 25760.51192 | | | |
| | (Incremental intercept) | | | | | |
| | 2.21E+04 | 1 | 22088.1 | | | |
| X | 9.53E+06 | 370 | | | | |

## 11. Transportations

| *Source* | *RSS* | *df* | *Mean Square* | *F(1)* | *F(2)* | *F(3)* |
|---|---|---|---|---|---|---|
| Z | 1910678.933 | 368 | 5192.062318 | 18.6 | 26.57 | 23.23 |
| | (Incremental Slope) | | | | | |
| | 137973.067 | 1 | 137973.067 | | | |
| X and D | 2048652 | 369 | 5551.902439 | | | |
| | (Incremental intercept) | | | | | |
| | 1.03E+05 | 1 | 103274 | | | |
| X | 2.15E+06 | 370 | | | | |

## 12. Miscellaneous

| *Source* | *RSS* | *df* | *Mean Square* | *F(1)* | *F(2)* | *F(3)* |
|---|---|---|---|---|---|---|
| Z | 19889700.05 | 368 | 54048.09796 | 4.91 | 100.36 | 53.3 |
| | (Incremental Slope) | | | | | |
| | 5424556.95 | 1 | 5424556.95 | | | |
| X and D | 25314257 | 369 | 68602.32249 | | | |
| | (Incremental intercept) | | | | | |
| | 3.37E+05 | 1 | 336992.41 | | | |
| X | 25651249.41 | 370 | | | | |

## 13. Non-food Item

| Source | RSS | df | Mean Square | F(1) | F(2) | F(3) |
|---|---|---|---|---|---|---|
| Z | 7492032.949 | 368 | 20358.78519 | 70.84 | 38.27 | 38.99 |
| | (Incremental Slope) | | | | | |
| | 779155.751 | 1 | 779155.751 | | | |
| X and D | 8271188.7 | 369 | 22415.14553 | | | |
| | (Incremental intercept) | | | | | |
| | 1.59E+06 | 1 | 1587977.3 | | | |
| X | 9859166 | 370 | | | | |

## NOTES


1. Sinha, R.P. (1966): An Analysis of Food Expenditure in India. *Journal of Farm Economics*, Vol. 48, No. 1 (Feb.,), pp. 113-123.
2. Prais, S.J. and H.S. Houthakker (1955): *The Analysis of Family Budgets.* Cambridge University Press.
3. Houthakker, H.S. (1957): An International Comparison of Household Expenditure Patterns, Commemorating the Centenary of Engel's Law. *Econometrica*, Vol. 25, No. 4 (Oct.), pp. 532-551.
4. Iyengar, N.S., L.R. Jain and T.N. Srinivasan (1968).: Economies of Scale in Household Consumption: *A Case Study. Indian Economic Journal*, 15, Econometric Annual, pp. 465-477.
5. Gupta, D.B. (1968): A Comparison of Consumption Patterns in Uttar Pradesh and Madras—A study of inter-regional variations with reference to India. *Indian Economic Review*, New Series, 3, pp. 129-144.
6. Maitra, T. (1969): *On Regional and Temporal Variation in Engel Curves in Rural India.* ISI Technical Report No. Econ/2/69.
7. Jain, L.R. and S.D. Tendulkar (1973): Analysis of Occupational Differences in Consumer Expenditure Patterns in India. *Sankhya*, Series B, Vol. 35(June), pp. 230-267.
8. Coondoo, Dipankor (1975): A Comparison of Consumer Expenditure Patterns of Indian Middle Class and Working Class Families. *Sankhya*, Vol. 37, Series C, Pt. 2, pp. 81-101.
9. Keynes, J.M. (1936).: *The General Theory of Employment, Interest and Money*. Macmillan, New York, 1936.
10. Further development of consumption function is elaborated in Chapter 1.
11. This is in line with the observation of Roy Choudhury (1968).
12. Chow, G.C.: Test of Equality Between Sets of Coefficients in Two Linear Regressions. *Econometrica*, Vol. 28, 1960, pp. 591-605.

# 6
# Major Findings and Conclusion

We have analyzed the pattern of household consumer expenditure in North-Eastern Region and Mizoram in particular. Engel's Law has been taken as the underpinning theoretical assumption of declining share of food as consumer's expenditure rises. In order to find the general applicability of the received theory, we classified the various consumption items into necessities, luxuries and semi-luxuries and estimated their respective expenditure elasticities. It has also been observed that for the different income classes, there have been changes in the consumption pattern leading to the creation of class difference. This points to the fact that certain consumption goods and services which are regarded as a luxury to one class becomes a necessity to other class.

In another context, this study has also attempted to examine the rural-urban difference in consumption behaviour. While an average city-dweller has been found to spend almost twice the amount his counterpart in rural areas did, we have also examined how much difference exists in terms of allocation of his budgets to key segments.

The main findings and observations are the following:

1. The trend of monthly per capita consumer expenditure (MPCE), as a measure of the standard of living, revealed the gradual improvement of the standard of living in North Eastern Region (NER). The MPCE, at constant price, of India as well as NER has increased continuously during the period between 1994-95 and 2005-06. Rural MPCE of NER has increased from Rs. 378.74 in 1994-95 to Rs. 1081.00 in 2005-06; while rural MPCE of India has increased from Rs. 309.43 to Rs. 624.53 during the same period. Similarly, urban MPCE have increased from Rs. 492.28 to Rs. 1875 in NER and from Rs. 508.07 to Rs. 1170 in India during the period from 1994-95 to 2005-06. Rural total expenditure increased at compound annual growth rate of 4.26 per cent and 2.70 per cent in NER and India respectively. Urban

expenditure also increased at annual compound growth rate of 6.68 per cent in NER and 4.04 per cent in India.

2. There is an increasing trend of rural-urban disparity with the increase in MPCE during the 10 years period under study. Rural per capita consumer expenditure as a percentage of urban per capita consumer expenditure (or ratio of rural MPCE to urban MPCE) in NER decreased gradually from 76.94 per cent in 1994-95 to 62.72 per cent in 2000-01 to 57.65 per cent in 2005-06 for consumer expenditure at current prices. In case of MPCE at constant price, it decreased from 77.34 per cent in 1994-95 to 57.60 in 2005-06. The same trend of rural-urban disparity has also been observed in India.
3. A structural changes in the consumer expenditure patterns is being observed in NER during the study period where the share of food items in total expenditure (at current prices) decreased from 63.80 per cent to 40.34 per cent in rural areas and from 56.84 per cent to 33.09 per cent in urban areas during the period between 1994-95 and 2005-06. In case of expenditure at constant price, the share of food items declined from 65.66 per cent to 38.27 in rural areas and from 58.71 per cent to 31.22 per cent in urban areas for the period from 1994-95 to 2005-06. The declining share of food items is accounted for by an increase in the share of nonfood items in the total expenditure.
4. On the basis of the 62nd NSS Round (covering the period 2005-06), urban per capita consumption is significantly higher than rural per capita consumption in all States of NER. Rural MPCE ranged from Rs. 753 in Tripura to Rs. 1728 in Nagaland; while urban MPCE ranged from Rs. 1081 in Manipur to Rs. 3158 in Nagaland. In conformity with the differences in MPCE the share of food items in total expenditure is higher in rural areas than in urban areas. The share of food items in rural MPCE varies from 35.2 per cent in Nagaland to 47.8 per cent in Tripura; while in urban areas it varies from 25.6 per cent in Nagaland to 41.2 per in Manipur. This result reflects the operational evidence of Engel's law of declining food share as income increase.
5. According to the data of our sample survey (July-August 2007), the average MPCE of Mizoram was Rs. 1971 in which the average MPCE for rural areas was Rs. 1151.26 and for urban areas Rs. 2731.8. At the same time, while average per capita monthly income (PMI) of the Mizoram was Rs. 2414.8, it was

Rs. 1237.5 in rural and Rs. 3506.7 in urban areas. If the differences are taken to estimate correctly, the average propensity to consume (APC), the result obtained comes to 0.82 for the entire population and 0.93 in rural areas and 0.78 in urban areas. The contention of the Absolute Income Hypothesis (AIH) of the declining APC with an increase in income is found to be true in the state.

6. In the data of our sample survey, the commodity group 'cereals, salt, sugar and edible oils' accounted for the largest share in both rural and urban areas of Mizoram; while 'clothing and housing' is the largest component of nonfood consumption in rural and urban areas.
7. An examination of six MPCE classes revealed that the share of food item decreased with an increase in the total consumer expenditure i.e. it is 55.3 per cent in the bottom class and 14.9 per cent in the top class. On the contrary, the share of 'clothing and housing' showed an increasing tendency with the total expenditure. Consequently, Engel's Law is found to hold true to the observation of the consumption pattern of various MPCE classes of Mizoram.
8. Analysis of inequality in consumer expenditure in Mizoram, on the basis of our sample survey data, revealed that more than 53 per cent of the rural population is with MPCE less than Rs. 840 and more than 34 per cent of the urban population has MPCE which is less than Rs. 1880. Inequality of consumer expenditure is found to be higher in urban areas than in rural areas. It is observed that more than half of the rural households who are in the lowest MPCE bracket accounts for 23.43 per cent of the total rural expenditure; whereas the top 10 per cent accounted for 31.19 per cent of rural consumption. At the same time, more than half of the urban population who are in the lower income bracket account for 31.43 per cent of the total consumer expenditure; whereas the top 13.4 per cent who are in the top MPCE bracket accounted for 50.51 per cent of the urban consumer expenditure.
9. The magnitude of calculated Gini Concentration Ratio revealed that (i) there is more concentration in urban consumption than in rural consumption, and (ii) there is more concentration in the consumption of non-food items than in food item in all areas of Mizoram.

10. Estimated expenditure elasticity for food items is less than unity for linear and double-log Engel's functions. Thus, the proportion of expenditure spent on food decreases with an increase in total consumer expenditure. Food is technically a necessity judging from the inelastic state of the demand for it. Further, the positive intercept terms of the food consumption function suggests that the increase in its price will act to mount the indebtedness of the poor. The elasticity of non-food, on the other hand, is more than unity implying that non-food may be, technically, regarded as luxury items in the state.
11. Category-wise analysis of food items revealed that 'cereals, salt, sugar and edible oils' group has the lowest elasticity. This indicates 'cereals; salt, sugar and edible oils' group forms the most important staple food in Mizoram. As the intercept term for this group is positive, the present investigation suggested that even a slight increase in the prices of these items would result in the indebtedness of the poor.
12. Category-wise analysis of non-food items indicated that the commodity groups of 'pan, tobacco and intoxicants' and health care are treated as necessities. While health care is a necessity encompassing the welfare needs of everybody, the fact that a large majority of the people still consume 'pan, tobacco and intoxicants' group which is injurious to health defies any logic of rational behaviour.
13. The items groups of education, transportations, 'clothing and housing', 'entertainment and telecommunications', and miscellaneous may be considered as luxury items as their estimated expenditure elasticities are greater than unity. The lower income and therefore lower consumption is evident from the spending on education, which is estimated at Rs. 98.57 a month in rural areas, compared to Rs. 300.53 a month in urban areas. Proper education, which is the key to human resource development, is beyond the reach of certain sections of the society. One of the main reasons for this is the emergence of private educational institutions and professional institutions.
14. An Analysis of Variance (ANOVA) test revealed that there is no significant inter-class difference in the consumption behaviour in Mizoram for the following groups: (i) pan, tobacco and intoxicants, (ii) education, and (iii) total non-food items.
15. Comparative analysis revealed that 'entertainments and

telecommunications' are luxury items for rural community, but it is necessity for urban community. Similarly, health care is luxury for rural households while it is necessity for urban households. The higher proportion of medical bill in rural areas is attributed to the poor sanitation and healthcare facilities provided in villages. Further, the facilities of enjoyment (like phones, television, etc) available in urban areas are not accessible to a number of rural households.

16. The analysis of the effect of household size on consumption pattern revealed that the elasticities of consumption are negative for all luxury items; while it is positive for all groups which are necessities. In other words, family size is found to be inversely proportional to the consumption of all luxury items. Further, elasticity of consumption on family size is most negative for the item which has the highest elasticity on total consumer expenditure or income.
17. Economies of scale in consumption with the increase in family size is being operative in the consumption expenditure on 'entertainment and telecommunications', 'clothing and housing', transportations, miscellaneous items, and total nonfood items; while diseconomies have been found in the consumption of all groups of food items and one nonfood group, 'pan, tobacco and intoxicants' in rural and urban areas of Mizoram. Moreover, it is observed that the consumption of the item group 'cereals, salt, sugar and edible oils' is more dependent on the number of persons in the family (family size) rather than income or total expenditure of the family.
18. An Analysis of Covariance (ANOCOVA) test between rural and urban areas resulted in the significant difference of overall consumption behaviour between rural and urban areas of Mizoram. However, category-wise analysis of items reveals that there is no significant difference in case of 'pan, tobacco and intoxicants' and education.
19. The marginal propensity to consume (MPC), at aggregative level, of Mizoram is 0.61 which indicates the income elasticity of consumption is less than unity (i.e. 0.74). It implies the ratio of consumption to income (or average propensity to consume) decrease with an increase in income. The hypothesis that the consumption increases with the increase in income but less than proportionately is found to be true in Mizoram. The average

propensity to consume is found to be less than marginal propensity to consume. This is in line with the contention of Keynesian Absolute Income hypothesis that MPC < APC. Further, the Chow Test proved the evidence of wide disparity of consumption behaviour between rural and urban areas at aggregative consumption functions. Thus, the MPC of rural areas (0.74) is significantly higher than urban MPC (0.56), which suggests that the responsiveness of consumption to the changes in income is greater in rural areas than in urban areas.

20. The saving rate or average propensity to save (APS) of the state is 0.18 (i.e. 18% of the total income). Urban saving rate is found to be higher than rural saving rate at 0.07 (i.e. 7%) and 0.22 (i.e. 22%) for rural and urban areas respectively.
21. The marginal propensity to save (MPS) in Mizoram is 0.39 and the estimated income elasticity of saving is more than unity (i.e. 2.12). Thus, APS is found to increase with the increase in income levels or saving is an increasing function of income. Further, the MPS of urban areas (0.44) is significantly higher than rural MPS (0.26). Accordingly, it may be concluded that urban households have a higher saving potential or saving habit than rural households.

## CONCLUSION

The present study gives operational evidence of Engel's Law and the broad applicability of Keynesian Absolute Income Hypothesis in the analysis of consumer behaviour in Mizoram. According to our sample survey data, the major share of household expenditure was accounted for by food, which manifests a characteristic of low-income economy.

Increase in per capita consumer expenditure at constant price, being observed in rural and urban areas of North-Eastern Region during the period of 1994-95 to 2005-06, reflect the continuous improvement of the standard of living in the region. However, the analysis of the trend of MPCE in NER revealed the continuously increasing gap between rural and urban areas in terms of consumption or income (since consumption is the proxy variable for income). Even after taking into account the price differentials to the tune of 25 per cent (i.e. urban is 25 per cent higher than rural MPCE), rural-urban differences are still considerable in NER.

In addition to the increasing gap between rural and urban areas, it has been found, from the analysis of the sample survey data, more than half of the rural households in Mizoram are in the lowest MPCE bracket implying that the majority of rural households are poor. In urban areas, it is estimated that more than one-third of the population are at the lower income bracket which implies that one-third of the urban population are poor. Thus, the present study suggested that poverty and the growing inequalities in income and consumption have been the major challenges before the State.

The autonomous consumption or intercept term of the estimated Engel's Curve for total food items is found to be positive which must be negative or near zero to ensure accessibility for all family. This indicates the dis-savings of the family who are at the lowest income bracket to maintain minimum food requirements. In addition to this, the intercept term of the estimated Engel's curve for the most important staple food item of Mizoram, 'cereals, salt, sugar and edible oils', is also found to be positive implying the need to spend the major portion of income, neglecting other important items like education, healthcare, housing etc, or dis-savings for the people who are at the lower income bracket to maintain the minimum food requirements. Therefore, even a slight increase in food price will act to mount the indebtedness of the poor families. This result called for the governmental intervention to regulate the prices and supply of the food items in the state to enable the poor to get the minimum food requirements.

Undesirable consumption behaviour being observed in Mizoram is the mass consumption of 'pan, tobacco and intoxicant', which has inelastic demand in all classes; the items included in the category are all injurious to health. At the same time, proper health care, the basic necessity of life, turned out to be luxury items of consumption in rural areas of Mizoram. It means the attainment of health care depends on family income indicating that a number of families are deprived of health care facilities. This is largely due to the poor sanitation and health care facilities provided in villages. From the view point of welfare economics, the government is required to treat health care facilities as public goods whose provision should be made through budgetary means. Such provisions are justified on account of market failure and the possibility of immense external benefit that should have accrued to the community.

Education, the key to human resource development, has been found to be luxury items of consumption in the State. That is, certain sections of the population in the State, particularly rural population, have financial problems to send their children to good educational institutions which are usually established in urban areas. Since this unhealthy trend of rural-urban difference in education will have serious impact on the society and the economy in the near future, present study suggested further research on this issue to help the government to choke out public policy measures.

Lastly, the estimated rural saving rate and saving propensity are very low comparing with urban rate. However, the investment multiplier as an inverse of saving propensity is higher in rural areas than urban multiplier; hence, any governmental policy measures for rural development by increasing public expenditures in the rural areas is expected to have greater impact on income generation and on the improvement of standard of living in rural areas.

# Bibliography


Ackley, Gardner (1978). *Macroeconomics: Theory and Policy.* New York: Macmillan.

Ahluwalia, I.J. (1979). *Behaviour of Prices and Outputs in India: A Macro-Econometric Approach.* Macmillan, Delhi.

Allen, R.G.D. and A.L. Bowley (1935). *Family Expenditure.* London Staples.

Ando, A. and F. Modigliani (1965). Velocity and the Investment Multiplier. *American Economic Review* (September).

Angevine, G.E. (1974). Forecasting Consumption with a Canadian Consumer Sentiment Measure. *Canadian Journal of Economics*, May, pp. 273-89.

Bailey, M.J. (1971). *National I7ncome and the Price Level.* McGraw Hill 2nd Ed.,

Bal, H.K. and H.S. Bal (1970). Expenditure Elasticities for Rural Punjab. *Indian Journal of Agricultural Economics*, Vol. 25, pp. 121-128.

Ball, R.J. and P.S. Drake (1964). The Relationship between Aggregate Consumption and Wealth. *International Economic Review*, Vol. V, pp. 63-81, January.

Battacharya, N. (1973). *The Average Elasticity of Variable Elasticity Engel Curve.* Technical Report No. Eco/2/73, Indian Statistical Institute, Calcutta.

Bhattachary, S.S., *et al.* (1980). *Between States Variation in Consumer Prices and Per Capita Household Expenditure Data.* Sarvekshana, Vol. III, No. 4, pp. 107-120.

Bhattacharya, N. and G.S. Chatterjee (1980). *A Further Note on Between State Variations in Level of Living in Rural India.* Technical Report No. NIRU/4/80 of Indian Statistical Institute, Calcutta.

Bhattacharya, N. and T. Maitra (1970). *An Analysis of Engel Curves Based on NSS Household Budget Data for 7th to 22nd Rounds.* Technical Paper at the 10th Indian Econometric Conference at Madurai.

Blaug, Mark (1996). *Economic Theory in Retrospect.* 5th Edition. Cambridge University Press, United Kingdom.

Blinder, A.R. and A. Deaton (1985). *Time Series Consumption Function Revisited.* Brookings Paper on Economic Activity, Vol. 2, pp. 465-521.

Blinder, A.S. (1975). Distribution Effects and the Aggregate Consumption Function. *Journal of Political Economy*, June, pp. 447-75.

Bodkin, R.G. (1959). Windfall Income and Consumption. *American Economic Review*, September. pp. 602-14.

Bodkin, R.G. (1963). Windfall Income and Consumption: *Comment. American Economic Review*, June, pp. 445-447.

Bojner, H. (1977). The Effect on Consumption of Household Size and Composition. *European Economic Review*, 9, pp. 169-193.

Bose, D.K. (1960). *Expenditure Consumption Curves for Some Selected Commodities*. Studies on Consumer Behaviour, Indian Statistical Series, No. 6, Asia Publishing House, Bombay and Statistical Publishing Society, Calcutta.

Brady, D.S. and H.A. Barber (1948). The Pattern of Food Expenditures. *Review of Economics and Statistics*, XXX, pp. 198.

Brown, A. and A. Deaton (1972). Models of Consumer Behaviour. *Economic Journal*, 82, No. 328.

Brown, J.A.C. (1954). *The* Consumption of Food in Relation to Household Composition and Income. *Econometrica*, Vol. 22, pp. 444-460.

Brown, T.M. (1952). Habit Persistence and Lags in Consumer Behaviour. *Econometrica*, Vol. 20, pp. 355-371.

Burk, Marguerite C. (1951). Changes in the Demand for Food from 1941 to 1950. *Journal of Farm Economics.* Vol. 33, No. 3 (Aug.), pp. 281-298.

Burk, Marguerite C. (1958). *An Appraisal of Changes in Rural Food Consumption.* Journal of Farm Economics, XL: 3:572-580, August.

Burk, Marguerite C. (1959). The Study of Regional Food Consumption. *Journal of Farm Economics*, XLI: 5:1040-1049, December.

Campbell, J. and N. Mankiw (1990). Permanent Income, Current Income and Consumption. *Journal of Business and Economic Statistics*, Vol. 8, pp. 265-279.

Chakravari, S.K. (1977). *Behaviour of Prices in India, 1952-70: An Empirical Study.* Macmillan, Delhi.

Chambers, M.J. (1991). *An Alternative Time Series Model of Consumption: Some Empirical Evidence.* Applied Economics, Vol. 23, pp. 1361-1366.

Chern, Wen S., *et al.*, (2002). *Analysis of Food Consumption Behaviour by Japanese Households.* Agriculture and Development Economic Division of the Food and Agriculture Organisation. Working Paper No. 206. www.fao.org/es/esa

Coondoo, Dipankor (1975) . A Comparison of Consumer Expenditure Pattern of Indian Middle Class and Working Class Families. Sankhya: *The Indian Journal of Statistics*. Vol. 37, Series C, Pt. 2, pp. 81-101.

Coondoo, Dipankor (1969) . *The Effect of Relative Prices on Engel Elasticity of Cereals in India.* Arthaniti, Vol. 12.

Coondoo, Dipankor, *et al.* (1981). Engel Curve Analysis with Non-Monetized Consumption. Journal of Income and Wealth, Vol. 5, No. 2, July.

Cranfield, John A.L., *et al.* (1998). Changes in the Structure of Global Food Demand. *American Journal of Agricultural Economics*, Vol. 80, No. 5, pp. 1042-1050.

Crockett, J. (1960). *Demand Relationships for Food, in* 'Study of Consumer Expenditure, Income and Savings'. 1, Ed. Friend and Jones, University of Pennsylvania.

Dandekar, V.M. and P. Venkataramaiah (1975). *Data Base of Indian Economy.* Vol. II, ed., The Indian Econometric Society, Hyderabad.

Davidson, J.E.H., *et al.*, (1978). Econometric Modelling of Aggregate Time Series Relationship between Consumers, Expenditure and Income in United Kingdom. *The Economic Journal*, Vol. 88, pp. 661-692.

Davis, M.A. (1984). The Consumption Function in Macroeconomic Models: A Comparative Study. *Applied Economics*, Vol. 16., pp. 799-838.

Davis, T.E. (1952). The Consumption Function as Tool for Prediction. *Review of Economic Statistics*, Vol. 34, pp. 270-77.

Deaton, A. (1986). *Life-cycle Models of Consumption: Is the Evidence Consistent with the Theory?.* National Bureau of Economic Research, Working Paper No. 1910.

Deaton, A. (1972). Wealth Effect on Consumption in a Modified Life Cycle Model. *The Review of Economic Studies*, Vol. 39, pp. 443-454.

Deaton, A. (1974). The Analysis of Consumer Demand in the United Kingdom, *1900-1970. Econometrica*, 42, No. 2, pp. 341-367.

Goreux, L.M. (1964). *Projection de la Demands des Prouits Agricoles on Europe Occidentale en 1970.* In 'Europe's Future Consumption' (ed.), J. Sandee, 2, North Holland Publishing Company, Amsterdam.

Deaton, A. and J. Muellbauer (1980). An Almost Ideal Demand System. *American Economic Review*, No. 70, pp. 312-336.

Desai, M.J. (1973). Macro Econometrics Models for India—*A Survey. Sankhya Series* B, (June)

Devendra, B. Gupta (1973). *Consumption Pattern in India.* Tata McGraw Hill Publishing Company Limited, New Delhi.

Doom, Van J. (1975). Aggregate Consumption and the Distribution of Incomes. *European Economic Review*, October, pp. 417-23.

Dowling, J, adn A. Lahiri (1986). *Growth, Structural Transformation and Consumption Behaviour: Evidence from Asia.* World Bank Discussion Paper, No. 200.

Duessenberry, James S. (1949). *Income, Saving and the Theory of Consumer Behaviour*. Harvard University Press, Cambridge, Massachusetts.

Economic Research Service/USDA (1997). *Cross-Country Analysis of Food Consumption Pattern.* Working Paper No. 01-1.

Evans, Michael K. (1967). The Importance of Wealth in the Consumption Function. *Journal of Political Economy,* Vol. 75, pp. 335-351, Part 1, April.

Farrel, M.J. (1959). The New Theories of the Consumption Function. *The Economic Journal*, Vol. 69, No. 276 (Dec.), pp. 678-696.

Farrel, M.J. (1954). Some Aggregation Problems in Demand Analysis. *Review of Economic Studies*, Vol. 21, pp. 193.

Ferber, R. (1953). *A Study of Aggregate Consumption Functions.* National Bureau of Economic Research, Technical Paper 8.

Flavin, M. (1981). The Adjustment of Consumption to Changing Expectations about Future Income. *Journal of Political Economy*, Vol. 89, No. 5, pp. 974-1009.

Forsyth, Findlay (1960). The Relationship Between Family Size and Family Expenditure. *Journal of the Royal Statistical Society*, Series A, 123, pp. 367-393.

Friedman, M. (1957). *A Theory of Consumption Function.* Oxford and IBH Publishing Co. New Delhi, 1970.

Friend, I. (1946). Relationship between Consumers' Expenditure, Savings and Disposable Income. *The Review of Economics and Statistics*, Vol. 28, pp. 208-15.

Friend, I. and I.B. Kravis (1957). *Consumption Patterns and Permanent Income. American Economic Review*, May, pp. 269-301.

Ganguly, A. (1960). *Consumption Pattern in Different Occupation Group.* Studies on Consumer Behaviour, Indian Statistical Series, No. 6, Asia Publishing House and Statistical Publishing Society, Calcutta.

Ghose, Suchismita and N. Bhattacharya (1995). Effect of Reference Period on Engel Elasticities of Clothing and Other Items: Further Results. Sankhya: *The Indian Journal of Statistics*, Vol. 57, Series B, Pt. 3, pp. 433-449.

Gilboy, E. (1938). The Propensity to Consume. *Quarterly Journal of Economics*, pp. 120-140, November.

Goreaux, L.M. (1957). *International Comparison of Engel Curves—Annex of Log-normal Adjustment of Engel Curves.* Paper submitted to the 19th European Congress of the Econometric Society, Luxembourg, August.

Goreaux, L.M. (1959). *Income Elasticity of the Demand for Food.* Rome, FAO, Mimeo.

Goreaux, L.M. (1960). Income and Food Consumption. *Monthly Bulletin of Agricultural Economics and Statistics*, No. 9, October, pp. 1-13.

Goreaux, L.M. (1973). *Consumption Patterns in India.* Tata McGraw Hill Publishing Company Limited, Bombay-New Delhi.

Government of India . *Reports of Households Consumption Expenditures.* Various Rounds of National Sample Survey of Organisation, Ministry of Statistics and Programme Implementation.

Government of Mizoram (2006). *Statistical Handbook 2006.* Directorate of Economics and Statistics.

Gupta, D.B. (1968). A Comparison of Consumption Patterns in Uttar Pradesh and Madras—A Study of Inter-regional Variations with Reference to India. *Indian Economic Review*, New Series, 3, pp. 129-144.

Gupta, D.B. (1973). *Consumption Patterns in India, A Study of Inter-regional Variations.* Tata McGraw-Hill Publishing Company Limited, Bombay-New Delhi.

Gupta, K.L. (1970). Income, Consumption and Saving in Urban and Rural India: *A Note. The Review of Income and Wealth*, Series 16, No. 4 (Dec.) pp. 377-388.

Haavelmo, T. (1947). Family Expenditures and the Marginal Propensity to Consumer. *Econometrica*, No. 15, October, pp. 335-341.

Haines, George H. (1969). *Consumer Behaviour Learning Models of Purchasing.* Jr. London: Collier-McMillan; New York: The Free Press.

Haitovsky, Y. (1968). An Efficient Estimation of Regression Equations Based on Classified Data When the Cross Classification are Unknown. *Review of Economic Studies*, 35, pp. 77-89.

Hall, R.E. (1978). Stochastic Implications of the Life Cycle Hypothesis: Theory and Evidence. *Journal of Political Economy, Vol. 86, pp. 971-987.*

Hood, W.C. (1955). Empirical Studies of Demand. *Canadian Journal of Economics and Political Science*, Vol. 21, pp. 309-327.

Houthakker, H.S. (1957). An International Comparison of Household Expenditure Patterns, Commemorating the Centenary of Engel's Law. *Econometrica*, Vol. 25, No. 4 (Oct.,), pp. 532-551.

Houthakker, H.S. (1958). The Permanent Income Hypothesis. *American Economic Review*, June, pp398.

Houthakker, H.S. (1960). *The Influence of Prices and Incomes on Household Expenditures.* Bulletin de 1' Institut International de Statistique 37(2): pp. 9-22.

Houthakker, H.S. (1961). The Present State of Consumption Theory. *Econometrica*, 29:4:704-740, October.

Houthakker, H.S. and L. Taylor (1970). *Consumer Demand in the USA, 1929-1970: Analysis and Projections.* Harvard University Press.

Iyengar, N.S. (1960). On a Problem of Increase on Consumer Demand. Sankhya-*The Indian Journal of Statistics*, Vol. 22, pp. 379-390.

Iyengar, N.S. (1960). On a Method of Computing Engel Elasticities from Concentration Curves. *Econometrica*, Vol. 28, pp. 882-891.

Iyengar, N.S. (1964). A Consistent Method of Estimating the Engel Curve from Grouped Survey Data. *Econometrica*, 32, pp. 591-618.

Iyengar, N.S. (1964). Contributions to Analysis of Consumer Expenditure. Unpublished Doctoral Dissertation, Indian Statistical Institute.

Iyengar, N.S. and S. Krishna Moorty (1959). On Some Econometric Models of India. *Arthaniti*, Vol. 2.

Iyengar, N.S. and L.R. Jain (1969). Projection of Consumption, Rural/ Urban India, 1970-71 and 1975-76. *Economic and Political Weekly*, 4, No. 48, November 29.

Iyengar, N.S. and L.R. Jain (1974). Changes in the Pattern of Consumption in India. *Arthavijnan*, 16, No. 3, pp. 231-266.

Iyengar, N.S. and N. Bhattacharya (1970). *Studies on Consumer Behaviour in India—A Survey of Research in Economics.* Econometrics, Vol. III, Allied Publishers, New Delhi.

Iyengar, N.S., *et al.*, (1968). Economies of Scale in Household Consumption: *A Case Study. Indian Economic Journal*, 15, Econometric Annual, pp. 465-477.

Johar, R.S. and H.S. Sandhu (1982). Consumption Pattern in Punjab. *The Indian Economic Journal*, Vol. 29, No. 4, pp. 69-85.

Jones, R.C. (1960). Transitory Income and Expenditures on Consumption Categories. *American Economic Review*, Vol. 50 (May,) pp. 584-92

Keynes, J.M. (1936). The General Theory of Employment, Interest and Money. New York: Harcourt, Brace.

Klein, L. (1947). The Use of Economic Models as a Guide to Economic Policy. *Econometrica*, Vol. 15, pp. 111-51.

Klein, L.R. and J.B. Lansing (1955). Decision to Purchase Consumer Durable Good. *Journal of Marketing*, XX:2:108-132, October.

Klein, L.R. and N. Liviatan (1957). *The Significance of Income Variability on Saving Behaviour.* Oxford University Institutes of Statistics, Bulletin. Vol. 19 (May,), pp. 151-60.

Koutsoyiannis, A. (1979). *Modern Microeconomics*. 2nd Edition, Macmillan, Hong Kong.

Kreinin, M.E. (1961). Windfall Income and Consumption—Additional Evidence. *American Economic Review*, Vol. 51 (June,), pp. 388-90.

Krishnamurthy, K. (1965). Consumption Function for India: *A Macro-time Series Study. Indian Journal Economic Journal*, 13, October-December, pp. 217-231.

Kuznets, Simon (1942). *Uses of National Income in Peace and War*. Occasional Paper 6, National Bureau of Economic Research, New York.

Kuznets, Simon (1946). *National Income: A Summary of Findings.* National Bureau of Economic Research. Princeton University Press, Princeton.

Laumas, Prem S. and Khan A. Mohabbat (1972). The Permanent Income Hypothesis: Evidence from Time-Series *Data. The American Economic Review*, Vol. 62, No. 4 (Sept.,) pp. 730-734.

Leser, C.E.V. (1941). Family Budget Data and Price-Elasticities of Demand. *The Review of Economic Studies*, Vol. 9, No. 1 (Nov.,) pp. 40-57.

Leser, C.E.V. (1963). Forms of Engel Functions. *Econometrica*, Vol. 31, No. 4 (October,), pp. 694-703.

Leser, C.E.V. (1962). *Demand Relationships for Ireland.* Economic Research Institute Paper No. 4, Dublin.

Liviatan, N. (1964). *Consumption Pattern of Israel, Jerusalem.* Academic Press Limited, Jerusalem.

Liviatan, N. (1961). Errors in Variables and Engel Curve Analysis. *Econometrica*, Vol. 29, pp. 336-362.

Mack, R. (1948). The Direction of Change in Income and Consumption Function. *Review of Economics and Statistics*, Vol. 30, pp. 239-258.

Mahajan, B.M. (1971). Inter-regional Homogeneity of Consumer Behaviour in India. *Arthavijnan*, Vol. 13, pp. 1-13.

Maitra, T. (1969). On Regional Temporal Variation of Engel Curves in Rural India. ISI Technical Report No. Econ/2/69.

Mammon, Thampy (1982). Consumption Function: Some Further Tests. *The Indian Economic Journal*, Vol. 30, No. 1 (July-Sept.) pp. 15-22.

Marshall, Alfred (1890). *The Principles of Economics.* 8th Edition, Macmillan, New York, 1948.

Mazumdar, Amita (1983). *Consumer Expenditure Pattern in India.* Technical Report No. ERU/17/83, Indian Statistical Institute, Calcutta.

Modigliani, F. and A. Ando (1963). The Life Cycle Hypothesis of Saving: Aggregate Implications and Tests. *American Economic Review*, Vol. 53, pp. 56-83.

Modigliani, F. and R.E. Brumberg (1954). *Utility Analysis and Consumption Function: An Interpretation of Cross section data.* Post Keynesian Economics, Rutgers University Press, pp. 388-436.

Molana, H. (1990). The Time Series Consumption Function: Error Correction, Random Walk and Steady State. *The Economic Journal*, Vol. 101, pp. 383-402.

Muellbauer, J. and R. Lattimore (1995). The Consumption Function: A Theoretical and Empirical Overview. *Handbook of Applied Econometrics*, Vol. 1: *Macroeconomics* edited by M.H. Wickens, Oxford.

Mukherjee, M., and D.S.P. Rao (1970). *Non-monetized Consumption in the Analysis of Consumer Behaviour.* ISI Technical Report, No. NIRU/7/70.

Mukherjee, M., and D.S.P. Rao (1974). *Consumer Behaviour in the Presence of Kind Income.* Unpublished Mimeo.

Nair, P.R.G. (1968). *Food Grains Price Policies in India, in Food Policy in India.* Indian Economic Association.

Narasimham, N.V.A. (1956). *A Short-Term Planning Model for India.* North Holland Publishing Co., Amsterdam.

Nisbet, Charles T. and Firouz Vakil (1972). Some Estimates of Prices and Expenditure Elasticities of Demand for Marijuana Among UCLA Students. *The Review of Economics and Statistics*, Vol. 54, No. 4 (Nov.), pp. 473-475.

Phillips, L. (1974). *Applied Consumption Analysis.* North Holland, Amsterdam.

Prais, S.J. and H.S. Houthakker (1955). *The Analysis of Family Budgets.* Cambridge University Press.

Prasad, A.R. (2001). *Consumption Behaviour in India: Theory and Evidence.* Reliance Publishing House, New Delhi.

Rao, C.R. (1972). *Data Base Indian Economy.* Vol. I, ed., The Indian Econometric Society, Hyderabad.

Reid, M. (1962). Consumption, Saving and Windfall *Gains. American Economic Review*, September, pp. 728-737.

Roy Choudhury, Uma Datta (1968). Income, Consumption and Saving in Urban and Rural India. *The Review of Income and Wealth*, Series 14, No. 1 (March,) pp. 37-56.

Roy, J. and S.K. Dhar (1958). *A Study of Pattern of Consumer Expenditure in Rural and Urban India.* ISI PD WP No. 101.

Roy, J., *et al.* (1960). *A Study of Concentration Curves as a Description of Consumption Pattern.* Studies on Consumer Behaviour, Asia Publishing House, London.

Roy, J., *et al.* (1960). *A Study on the Pattern of Consumer Expenditure in Rural and Urban India.* Indian Statistical Series, No. 6, Calcutta, Indian Statistical Institute.

Rudra, A. (1972). *Survey of Research on Consumption, Saving and Capital Formation.* The Data Base of Indian Economy. Indian Econometric Society, New Delhi.

Rudra, A. (1976). *Consumption, Savings and Capital Formation.* A Trend Report, in Lakdawala, D.T. (ed.), A Survey of Research in Economics, Vol. 2, Macro-economics,(ICSSR Project), Allied Publishers, New Delhi, pp. 47-123.

Rudra, A. and B. Roy (1960). *Some Results in Consumption Studies on Consumer Behaviour.* Asia Publishing House, London.

Saha, Somesh (1980). Some Further Estimates of Engel Elasticities for Rural and Urban India. Sankhya, *The Indian Journal of Statistics*, Series D, Vol. 42, Parts 1, pp. 127-150.

Singh, Amarjit and Haramol Singh (1971). Changing Consumption Pattern In Punjab: Projections of Consumer Demand for 1973-74. *Economic and Political Weekly*, Vol. VI, No. 50.

Singh, Balbir (1969). *A Study of Consumption Function,* Unpublished Ph.D, Thesis of the University of Delhi.

Singh, Balbir and Ramesh C. Kumari (1971). *The Relative Income Hypothesis—A Cross Country Analysis.* The Review of Income and Wealth, Series 17, pp. 341-348.

Sinha, R.P. (1966). An Analysis of Food Expenditure in India. *Journal of Farm Economics*, Vol. 48, No. 1 (Feb.), pp. 113-123.

Stigler, George J. (1954). The Early History of Empirical Studies of Consumer Behaviour. *The Journal of Political Economy*, Vol. LXII, April, pp. 95-113.

Stone, R. (1954). Linear Expenditure Systems and Demand Analysis: *An Application to the Pattern of British Demand. Economic Journal*, Vol. 54, pp. 511-527.

Theil, Henri., *et al.*, (1989). *International Evidence on Consumption Patterns.* Greenwich, CT: JAI Press Inc.,

Upender, M. (1994). Estimation of Propensity to Save. *Finance India*, Vol. VIII, No. 2, June.

Upender, M. (1996). The Short and Long Run Aggregate Consumption Functions. *Indian Journal of Applied Economics*, Vol. 5, No. 2, January-March.

Upender, M. (1998). Estimates of Expenditure Elasticities of Demand. *Finance India*, Vol. XII, No. 3, September.

Upender, M. (1999). Expenditure Elasticity for Clothing. *Anvesak*, Vol. 29, December.

Varian, Hal R. (2005). *Revealed Preference.* www.ischool.bekerly.edu/~hal/Papers/2005/revpref.pdf.

Wold, H.O.A. (1953). *Demand Analysis.* John Wiley and Sons Inc., New York.

Working, H. (1943). Statistical Laws of Family Expenditure. *Journal of the American Statistical Association*, Vol. 38, pp. 43-56.

Woytinsky, W.S. (1948). *Consumption-Saving Function.* The Review of Economics and Statistics, Vol. 30, No. 1, February, pp. 45-56.

Yang, Charles Yneu (1964). An International Comparison of Consumption Functions. *The Review of Economics and Statistics*, Vol. 46, No. 3 (Aug.,) pp. 279-286.

Zeldes, S.P. (1989). Consumption and Liquidity Constraints: An Empirical Investigation. *Journal of Political economy*, Vol. 97, pp. 305-345.

Zellner, Arnorld (1957). *The Short-Run Consumption Function. Econometrica*, Vol. 25, No. 4 (Oct.,) pp. 552-567.

# Index